Dog-Friendly
DOG TRAINING

Andrea Arden

Dog-Friendly
DOG TRAINING

Illustrations by Tracy Dockray

Howell Book House

Hungry Minds, Inc.
909 Third Avenue
New York, NY 10022
www.hungryminds.com

For general information on Hungry Minds' products and services please contact our Customer Care Department within the U.S. at 800-762-2974, outside the U.S. at 317-572-3993 or fax 317-572-4002.

ISBN: 1-58245-009-9

Library of Congress Catalog Card Number: 99-62835

Book Design by George J. McKeon
Cover Design by Michael Freeland

Contents

For my brother George.

Acknowledgments

I am lucky to count myself among the thousands that have been influenced by Dr. Ian Dunbar. If one were to count up the hours that Dr. Dunbar has spent helping people learn a better, kinder way of teaching dogs, I have no doubt they would find that he has given up years of his life in this effort.

Thankfully, it has not been in vain. Because of him, dog training is fun, friendly and full of tail wags.

Enormous thanks goes to my editor, Amanda Pisani. Brains, tact, humor and patience, what a perfect mix for an editor of dog books!

Thanks also to Elaine, Laura and John who were incredibly understanding and supportive while I lost my mind writing two books at once!

Last but not least, thanks to Oliver, Meggie and all of the dogs who have made my life what I dreamed it would be when I was a child.

What Is Dog-Friendly Dog Training?

When it comes to the best way to train your dog, the sheer wealth and breadth of conflicting advice is often bewildering. Bookstores and pet shops exhibit a vast array of literally hundreds of different dog books and each one recommends different dog training methods. Jerk the leash, don't jerk the leash, use food, don't use food, always do this, never do that.

Worse yet, for the longest time most people have associated dog training with choke collars and leash jerks, assuming the whole process to be a chore and a drag. Wrong, wrong, wrong! An incredible rediscovery has been made in the field of dog training: Training your dog is fun! And, better yet, the more fun you and your dog have while training, the faster and more effective training becomes.

Luckily for today's dogs, the popularity of reward-based training has grown steadily through the 1980s and '90s and has become the dog-friendly revolution of the next millenium.

Dog-friendly dog training is the best way to create the dog of your dreams.

In a nutshell, dog-friendly dog training focuses on three things:

1. Rewarding Good Behaviors

2. Preventative Management

3. Using Gentle Methods to Teach

FOCUSING ON REWARDING GOOD BEHAVIORS

There are two objectives in training your dog; a major objective and a minor objective. The all-important major objective of friendly, intelligent pet dog training centers on teaching dogs *to do* things we want them to do. The secondary and minor objective is to teach dogs *not to do* things we do not want them to do.

Dog-friendly dog training zeroes in on the major objective, teaching your dog what you want and rewarding him for doing so. This is the easiest way to train your dog. After all, there aren't that many things we consider "right" for pet dogs to do, so you really don't have that many things to teach. On the other hand, there is an endless list of "wrong" things that pet dogs can do. And so, trying to train by punishing your dog for each mistake would be a very lengthy and unpleasant process for both you and your dog.

For any natural doggy behavior you can come up with, there are lots of inappropriate outlets and usually just a few right choices. For example, imagine the one "right" spot for your dog to use as his doggy toilet (either outside or on paper) and imagine how nice and easy it is to take him to that spot when he needs to go (and reward him for

Teaching Right Is Easier than Teaching Wrong

Rewarding good behavior is the central tenet of successful dog-friendly training. Choosing to focus on rewards rather than punishments is the most important decision you will make with respect to educating your dog. Not only is doing so more fun (for you and your dog) but it is also much easier. After all, there is a rather short list of Right behaviors, but an almost endless list of Wrong behaviors.

"Right" Doggy Behaviors

sitting to greet people

walking nicely on leash

playing nicely with people

playing with doggy toys (especially stuffed chewtoys)

lying down calmly

eliminating in the doggy toilet (outside or inside on paper)

playing nicely with other dogs

responding to your requests

"Wrong" Doggy Behaviors

jumping up on visitors

pulling on the leash

playing roughly with people

raiding the garbage

barking for long periods

chewing on your toys (cds, books, the remote)

chasing the cat

eliminating in the house (in hundreds of different spots)

fighting with other dogs

not responding to your requests

running away

digging in your garden

eating your food off the table

chewing on your shoes

chewing on your clothes

chewing on your furniture

chewing on plants

. . . add your dog's annoying behaviors here:

_____

_____

doing so). Now, imagine the hundreds of wrong places to urinate and how long it would take to punish your dog for going in each of those spots. Likewise, picture your house after your dog has tried out all of the "wrong" things to chew. Now, imagine how much easier it would have been if you had just gotten him hooked on a chewtoy.

Catch Your Dog Doing Something Right!

It may be just human nature, but we tend to ignore good behavior and instead focus most of our attention on behaviors we don't like. Try to catch your dog doing something right at least five times a day and you'll find that each day it will be easier and easier to do so, because your dog will be learning the best ways to get your attention. For example, if he walks up to you and sits in front of you let him know how pleased you are that he chose such a polite and friendly way to say hello.

Why else is rewarding good behavior so important? For the simple fact that once you have successfully taught your dog how you would like him to behave, he no longer misbehaves. And when he doesn't misbehave, there is no reason to punish him. Do yourself and your dog a favor, the first day your dog comes home with you—start teaching your dog what you want him to do. And if you already have a dog … start today!

You'll have a whole lot of cleaning to do after you've allowed your dog to test out all the wrong places to go to the bathroom.

Teaching your dog the one right spot to go to the bathroom is so much easier than punishing him for going in innumerable wrong places.

The principle of teaching "what is right" from the outset makes special sense developmentally—in other words, during puppyhood. Not even 20 years ago it was impossible to enroll your dog in obedience classes until he was *at least* six months old. This would be similar to keeping children out of school until their late teens! By six months of age, most uneducated dogs were seriously out of control and required some physically rigorous and mentally demanding training methods.

Thankfully, times have changed: Puppy training is widely available and trainers, veterinarians, shelter workers and breeders encourage new dog owners to teach their dogs starting on the first day they take them home.

PREVENTATIVE MANAGEMENT

Rewarding your dog for being right is undoubtedly easier and more effective than punishing him for being wrong. Moreover, you can speed up the process by responsibly managing your dog's life to maximize the likelihood your dog will be right. This way, much of training becomes effortless, errorless learning and the need for harsh correction or punishment is simply unnecessary. Simple and smart.

You should be especially concerned with management until training takes effect. For example, until you have taught your dog to have a chewtoy habit, he should not be given unsupervised access to your home.

There are two parts to management: controlling the resources and controlling the environment.

Dogs are masters at training us to do all sorts of things for them. Try to remember that you decide when it's dinnertime, playtime, and time to go for a walk.

You Control the Resources

Doggy resources include anything your dog likes: food (normal kibble as well as special treats), praise from people (verbal and physical), life rewards (going for a walk, getting up on the couch, a ride in the car), toys and play (games with you or just chewing a toy).

Most owners give their dog free access to just about everything that is valuable to the dog. In fact, dogs are often rewarded with resources when they are doing things the owner doesn't like! For example, the dog jumps around like a madman as his food is being prepared and then the owner puts the bowl down for the dog to eat. Or the dog pulls on leash and the owner continues the walk. It's so much smarter to take control of these resources and use them to teach your dog to behave appropriately.

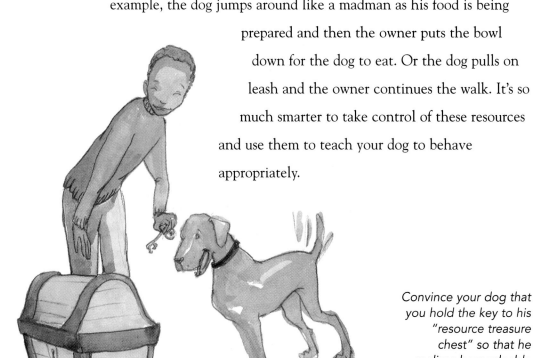

Convince your dog that you hold the key to his "resource treasure chest" so that he realizes how valuable you are, and how important it is to do as you ask.

Attention Please

A result of controlling the things your dog wants is that you will get his attention and this is crucial if you intend to teach him. When your dog pays attention to you (and then follows your instructions) he has an opportunity to have you unlock the door to get to all the things he loves.

Controlled access to a limited commodity increases its value. It's all a matter of supply and demand. If something is easily accessible and in great supply, the demand usually isn't so great. Consequently, make your dog's resources more valuable by controlling them. For example, go around and pick up your dog's toys and ask him to come, sit or lay down before you give him one to play with. Each time he comes up to you for some petting ask him to do something before you comply. When you serve him his dinner, ask him to do something before you put his bowl on the ground. Better yet, every once in a while sit down and hand feed him some of his meal and ask him to do something for *each* piece of kibble.

Similarly, when walking your dog on leash, regularly stop and wait for your dog to look at you and to sit before you continue walking. He will quickly learn that watching you and sitting when you stop is the way for the walk to continue. Let your dog know that you have what he wants and if he wants it, he just needs to ask, in this case, by sitting by your side when you stop.

A Working Dog Is a Happy Dog

No matter what your dog's size, he still needs a job to feel fulfilled and to achieve his full potential as a dog.

Don't feel badly about asking your dog to do a little something in return for resources. Unlike most of us, dogs love to have a job to do. Most pet dogs have no job, and in turn they have a very boring existence. You, however, can change all that.

You Control the Environment

By preparing your house in such a way that your dog does not have access to areas where he might make mistakes, you are essentially putting the odds in your dog's favor that he will be right. Doing this from the outset with your new puppy or dog will avoid predictable behavior problems and the potential need for punishment. This is also the best way to prevent further problems with your current dog.

Controlling your dog's access to areas where he might get into trouble is known in the dog training trade as the "shut the door" notion. For example, if your dog is getting into the garbage in the kitchen, shut the kitchen door, or get a garbage can that locks. If your dog is urinating in your bedroom, shut the bedroom door. Better yet, confine your dog to one room in the house. If you confine your

How can this dog not misbehave? The only options he has to occupy his time are ones that will annoy his owner! Creating a dog-friendly home, one in which he has very little opportunity to make mistakes, is one of the kindest things you can do for your dog.

dog to one room of the house, there are a thousand wrong things he can't do in the other rooms. This is essentially the same way we teach young children to behave in the home. You wouldn't consider allowing a toddler to roam around unsupervised.

You can also keep your dog on leash at your side. Doing so prevents so many problems that it would take a whole book to write them down. If you keep your dog on leash he can't chew inappropriate things, eliminate in the wrong places, etc. This is, of course, a temporary but necessary aspect of training. Once the dog has learned good habits, there is a whole lifetime of freedom in the home ahead.

Set Him Up to Be Right

Stack the deck in your dog's favor, so that he can not fail but to be right. If done properly, he should have no alternative but to behave in the way that you would like. For example, leave your dog in a crate, or a protected room, with three stuffed chewtoys and you are pretty much assured that your dog will quickly learn to enjoy chewing chewtoys rather than a whole host of other inappropriate household articles. He can't be destroying your house or barking incessantly if he is engrossed with his chewtoys.

Using Gentle Methods

When teaching your dog to respond on cue, he learns the Antecedent (cue, request, or command) signals that a Consequence (reward) is likely following the appropriate Behavior. These are the ABCs of teaching, Antecedent - Behavior - Consequence.

The reward (Consequence) causes the behavior to increase in frequency. For example, simply giving your dog a piece of kibble every time he sits quickly produces a "sit-happy" dog who sits more frequently. The reward also reinforces the association between the request and the response, such that the dog learns sitting when requested often produces rewards. The dog also learns that sitting at other times does not necessarily produce rewards. Ultimately, the dog learns to want to sit on request.

The above training sequence represents an oversimplification of Learning Theory—the Science of Dog Training. Your dog is going to learn very quickly if you present the ABCs.

Brain or Brawn?

Brain power is far superior to physical power when it comes to dog training (and just about everything else as a matter of fact!). Instead of trying to master difficult, time-consuming and largely ineffective physical methods to punish your dog for countless wrongs, why not just teach your dog what you want him to do using reward techniques? It is so much easier and quicker and a darn sight more enjoyable for you as well as your dog.

Almost everybody, including children, can train with their brain, but few people can master the rigors of physical training methods.

The Art of Dog Training though, depends very much on the skill of predicting, or causing the behavior we are trying to put on cue and increase in frequency. For example, when we ask the dog to sit, how do we know that the dog will sit so that we can reward him for doing so?

How the you go about this is the main determinate of the efficiency and effectiveness of training. Basically, there are just three techniques to predict or cause specific behaviors:

1. luring behavior (Lure/Reward training),

2. simply waiting for the behavior to happen on its own (Reward training), and

3. physically prompting the behavior.

As a dog-friendly trainer you will primarily use numbers 1 and 2, gentle Lure/Reward and Reward methods, to entice your dog to do things your way. Everyone, including children can easily master these two quick and fun ways to train. On the other hand, physical prompting methods aren't appropriate for all dogs and all people. A child certainly should not be expected to physically prompt a dog to get him to obey. Even adults may be at risk if they resort to pushing and pulling some dogs.

Lure/Reward Training

Lure/Reward training is a hands-off method to lure your dog into doing what you want him to do and then to reward him for doing it. Kibble from the dog's normal, daily diet is perhaps the best way to lure, but tennis balls or stuffed chewtoys also work well. You can entice your dog to move his nose, which gives you control over the dog's entire body, by moving a small lure. By manipulating the lure, you can:

- modify the dog's body position (sit, down, stand, rollover);
- modify the dog's direction of movement (come here, go to);
- get him to focus on specific objects (chewtoys, tennis balls, you) and
- even modify natural canine behaviors (chewing, digging, and barking).

Using Lure/Reward training, anyone, regardless of age or physical strength can position any size dog.

For example, ask your dog, "Do you like training too?" and then move a piece of kibble up and down in front of your dog's nose and magically he will nod his head in agreement. Then, offer the kibble lure as a reward for agreeing with you!

Lure/Reward training is the most effective way to get your dog to enjoy training and the trainer. Lure/Reward training has numerous beneficial side effects, but the best is that it teaches your dog to like all types of people, especially children, men and strangers. Dogs quickly learn to enjoy the company of anyone who takes the time to ask them to come, sit, lay down and rollover. Most importantly, Lure/Reward methods offer an easy, non-confrontational means for children to commandeer respect from the dog and train him to be happily and willingly compliant. Obviously, children can not physically force a dog to do anything, but with Lure/Reward training children can exert mental control.

All reward-training techniques have advantages, and a great advantage is that the dog can be trained from the outset without the aid of a leash. Therefore, the owner quickly establishes effective off-leash, distance control. Because of its speed and gentleness, Lure/Reward training is almost always the method of choice.

Reward Training

Reward training is very simple: you just wait for the right behavior to occur spontaneously before rewarding the dog. Generally,

What If My Dog Doesn't Like Food?

If your dog is completely disinterested in the food lure, teach him to thoroughly enjoy food by hand-feeding him for a few days. In the meantime, interact with your dog using what he does like, such as praise, affection, balls, toys, games, and activities. For example, use your hand to lure the dog to sit and invite him on the couch as a reward. Or use a tennis ball to lure him to come, but pet and praise as a reward. However, because food Lure/Reward training is so effective it would be a smart prospect to train your dog to like kibble—just ask your dog to eat one piece of kibble before each and every enjoyable activity. Before putting your dog on leash, before opening the door, every few steps when walking your dog, before letting him off leash, before throwing a tennis ball, before inviting him up on the couch. In just three days your dog will love kibble. Now, back to Lure/Reward training.

Reward training takes more time than Lure/Reward training, particularly at the beginning. When you start, you are waiting for the dog to behave appropriately, and it usually takes him a few "guesses" to get it right.

During Reward training, your dog will make many "mistakes," but each unrewarded "mistake" is important because it allows your dog to eliminate yet another unprofitable option. The more "mistakes," the more your dog learns what is *not* rewarding. Eventually your dog will hit upon what you want and the immediately rewarded behavior will soon be repeated many times. Dogs love playing this game.

For example, to train a dog to sit, take hold of a few pieces of kibble, stand still and wait for your dog to sit. He will go through a

Reward training techniques are extremely effective, which is why they are now used almost exclusively for training bomb-detection, search and rescue dogs and top-notch obedience competition dogs. They produce a reliable, happy dog.

whole repertoire of behaviors, like jumping up and barking. Ignore all of this and wait for the sit, he will do so eventually. Say "Good dog," offer him a piece of kibble and then do it again (you might have to take a step to get your dog to stand up). You will find your dog sits more and more quickly each time. Soon, your dog will develop the notion of sitting by your side when you stand still. Now you can predict when he will sit and say the word before he does so.

This is a good technique for teaching all-or-none behaviors (like sit and down) to rambunctious and easily distracted dogs. It is also an excellent technique to train your dog to pay attention. More complicated behaviors are shaped by rewarding the dog for successive approximations to the desired behavior, (when it's not exactly what you want but it's close). Used in this way, it is a truly wonderful technique for teaching more complicated behaviors like a retrieve or a fancy trick.

Anybody can Reward train, from anywhere, even when relaxing in an armchair. Reward training is great for all types of trainers, especially children and the elderly and it is wonderful for all types of dogs, especially the difficult ones, including fearful and aggressive dogs. In

When to Begin Training?

Now! Right away! Using dog-friendly methods it is never too early to train a puppy or a newly adopted adult dog. If you are planning to get a dog, read on. Reading this book will help you make an educated choice for the best education for you and your dog.

fact, reward training is the method of choice for active and excitable adolescent dogs. It calms dogs more quickly than any other method. You just ignore the adolescent antics and wait for the dog to do something good. It's the quickest way to train an adolescent dog to pay attention and to walk on leash calmly and to automatically sit when you stop.

Reward training methods are very calming. There is no need to be upbeat and exciting. Instead you can relax and enjoy watching your dog. Moreover, since you give no commands at the beginning, no one has any idea what you are trying to do and so you can not look stupid if your dog does not quickly do what you have in mind! Don't worry though, in no time at all everyone will know exactly what you are doing as they look on in amazement.

Physical Prompting

For years, dog training has been pretty much synonymous with leashes and collars. The very notion of dog training conjured up visions of a

Physical prompting requires that you have the requisite strength and agility to physically position your dog.

trainer expertly jangling the dog's collar with the leash to motivate him to heel, or gently tugging upwards on the leash and firmly pushing down on the dog's rump to place him in a sit. Physical Prompting seems at first to be extremely efficient and effective because the dog appears to respond promptly. However, Physical Prompting is deceptively complicated and it usually takes an experienced trainer to shine.

To manipulate a leash and gently handle a dog really takes a certain amount of talent and experience. These methods require physical strength to push, pull and jerk; great timing so you administer corrections at exactly the right moment; absolute consistency so that your dog learns that punishments are always an option; and an excellent understanding of dog behavior so that you lessen the chances of getting hurt by a dog who fights back. One of the biggest flaws in dog training methodology is that many trainers underestimate their own expertise. What comes so easily to them after 25 years of experience just falls apart in the hands of a novice owner working a novice dog.

When done correctly, with gentleness and patience, hands-on prompting encourages owners to do one of the most important things in pet ownership—to get their hands all over their dogs in a friendly, structured way. Hands-on prompting can be a good way to train, because teaching a dog to enjoy handling is so important. Be sure to offer plenty of food rewards to facilitate Physical Prompting. Touch your dog and give him a treat. Touch him for a longer time and offer another treat and so on. Eventually you will have a dog who thoroughly enjoys being touched, handled and even manhandled.

Note the importance of using Physical Prompting as a gentle handling and teaching technique. Few of us will succeed by jerking our dogs around. And if you're working with a fearful or aggressive dog, hands-on training can result in a disaster.

Friendly training methods have been used for years to train dolphins, whales and grizzly bears. After all, you can't very well put a choke collar on a whale and jerk him around a tank to get him to do want you want. If we can train these animals with friendly methods, we can certainly train our pet dogs the same way!

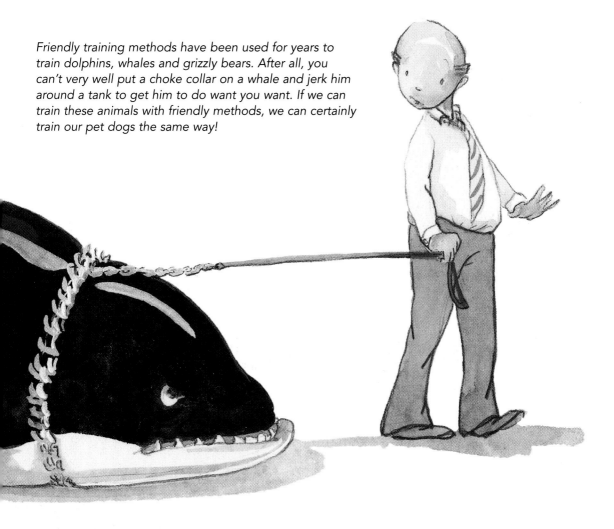

THE FOUR E'S OF TRAINING

Lure/Reward Training

EASE This is the easiest method to master and almost everybody in the family can do it. All you have to do is keep your hand steady and move the lure gently to entice the dog to assume different positions. You can even keep your other hand in your pocket, or behind your back.

EFFICIENCY   The use of the lure in training is almost magical: an untrained puppy or adult dog can be lured into a sit, down, or stand and in fact into any body position, in no time at all. Lure/Reward training is *very* fast. It is the quickest way to train any animal. And it is the quickest way to train any animal to do things quickly. Lure/Reward training is the method of choice for a good 95 percent of the things you want to teach your dog.

EFFECTIVENESS   One of the most effective training techniques. Because of the sheer speed and enthusiasm of the dog's responses, it is possible to practice hundreds of responses in a single training session, which makes it easy to objectively evaluate the dog's performance and to progressively test for better reliability.

ENJOYMENT Lure/Reward trained dogs have fun and their enthusiasm is infectious. Lure/Reward techniques have re-energized dog training. What used to be boring, mundane and repetitive has now become thrilling and exciting.

Reward Training

EASE Talk about easy. This is the time to relax and meditate. Make sure to take this book along so you have something to read while you wait. After the first one or two rewarded responses, things start to move at a quicker pace and it no time at all the dog's performance is improving in leaps and bounds before your very eyes.

EFFICIENCY Reward training is like getting on a roller coaster. The ride up seems long, but then but then it takes off at a lightning pace.

EFFECTIVENESS Reward training produces a highly reliable performance after just a single session. And over time, the reliability is enhanced, because Reward training increases the dog's attentiveness. This method is ideal for all family members to work with all types of dogs, especially the rambunctious and unruly ones. In fact the more rambunctious and inattentive the dog, the better the effect.

ENJOYMENT Everyone (dogs included), loves Reward training. Certainly one of the most enjoyable things about Reward Training is demonstrating it to others. Of all the techniques in dog training, Reward Training has the highest feel-good factor, since you'll feel an amazing connection with your dog. As your dog learns to pay attention to your body language and to read every nuance of your intention movements, you'll soon get the feeling that your dog is looking at you like you are his sun, moon and stars!

Physical Prompting

EASE Physical methods are difficult for many owners, especially children, to master. Many novice owners understandably become frustrated in their attempts to master apparently simple techniques, which actually require considerable patience and precision. They are best employed by experienced trainers, but are not really suitable for family training.

EFFICIENCY Physical Prompting is deceptive because initially it appears that the dog is learning quickly. And he does. He quickly learns to sit when touched on the collar or rump for example. However, it is not until the dog is off-leash in the park that you learn you have barely started training. If your ultimate goal is distance control, Physical Prompting methods will double up on your training time because you still have to teach the dog to respond to verbal commands off-leash.

EFFECTIVENESS Physical Prompting techniques often give the appearance that the dog is better trained than he is. The dog looks good on-leash but acts as if he has never been trained when released. In fact, the more you physically prompt the dog during early training, the harder it will be to achieve off-leash reliability later on.

ENJOYMENT With an experienced trainer, Physical Prompting techniques can be very pleasant experience for both dog and trainer, pretty much on par with ballroom dancing for people. Unfortunately, few owners successfully mimic the trainer's expertise and the gentle

Physical Prompting with hands and leash as demonstrated in class, often ends up as frustrated pushing and pulling (when copied by family members,) which dampens the enjoyment quotient.

TRAINING TECHNIQUES GO FULL CIRCLE

Up until the last century, dog training was a pretty friendly affair. Dogs were predominantly trained off leash using reward methods. And of course, if we go even farther back in time, food and gentleness was the way we lured the wolf into the human family.

Unfortunately, the 1900s brought with it an array of confusing punishment-based dog training techniques, and "correct me if I'm

Dogs were first lured into our lives using food and kindness.

wrong," became the mantra for the unassuming pet dog. Jerking on choke chains, yelling commands and other menacing tactics became the hallmarks of popular, unfriendly dog training methods. These techniques were harsh and demanding for both dogs and owners. Indeed, most dog owners found that the physical demands of these techniques were all but impossible to master. To better understand the dog-friendly approach, you need to understand where these punitive methods came from.

We're in the Army Now!

Perhaps pet dog trainers looked to military training methods for guidance. Obviously, military training techniques were intentionally harsh in an effort to weed out more sensitive dogs in the preliminary training, rather than having them break down in the field. Now, of course, most well-trained military dogs are trained using toys and treats. So, fun and friendly dog training has even invaded the military!

And Now We're in the Woods?

The second factor that led to unfriendly, punishment-based training is an attempt to adopt the way wolves communicate to the human training repertoire. This approach is severely flawed.

First, you don't look, smell or growl like a dog, and you don't wear a furry costume and crawl around on all fours. The point is, it is impossible for people to accurately communicate in dog language.

Moreover, wolves and dogs have an extremely complicated social structure that is composed of a number of flexible hierarchies. As a dog owner, an attempt to replicate this environment by attributing "alpha status" to yourself is a simplistic approach doomed to failure. Working from the premise that wolf mothers teach their young using severe physical corrections, an adversarial, combative training methodology was devised. Rather than teaching our best friends, we were advised to physically dominate our dog to bring him into line.

In actuality, however, very little physical force is required to maintain the stability of the social pack. Cooperation and passive gestures ensure that each member has access to resources (such as food). If you really want to act like a wolf, forget the growling and scruff shaking. Simply get control of the resources in your dog's life and show your dog what he should do to get them (i.e. sit, down, come when called, eliminate outside).

The Leash: A Good Tool Gone Bad

Yes, this simple, useful and very important training tool has had some unexpected and long lasting negative side effects.

A mere 50 years ago many dogs lived in areas where they could safely be off leash, but now the increased population density necessitates that dogs are walked on leash. Rather than developing the notion of staying close (the most important aspect of any relationship), the dog was *kept* close by the means of a leash. Additionally, the leash also made it easy to jerk the dog around and soon leash jerks became the universal correction almost to the exclusion of people using their intelligence and creativity in training. Indeed, the easy implementation of punishment is a major reason why leash training has gained such a bad reputation over the years. The final result—dogs that didn't respond well to being bullied wound up being labeled stupid, stubborn or dominant.

PUPPIES SAVE THE DAY!

As people became dependent on physical and punitive training methods, it became impossible to train puppies. After all, you don't want to jerk, push and pull a puppy do you? So, people were advised to wait to train their puppies until they were six months old and could withstand the rigors of training. I certainly agree that puppies do not do well with punishment-based methods, but then neither do most adult dogs!

This of course is disastrous! Scientists have long realized how crucial a dog's early weeks of life are and suggested that waiting to train until a dog was all but grown is just plain silly. Not training puppies made matters even worse because by the time they hit adolescence they were out of

Puppies prompted the turn around to the friendly, positive direction of yesteryear. Gentle methods of training used to teach young puppies were so much fun and so effective that people began to use them with adult dogs.

control and owners were at their wits end, resorting to almost any means, especially punishment, to get control. Ironically, when they began to train their adolescent dog they used the same harsh methods they originally avoided by not training at all!

Thanks go to veterinarian, animal behaviorist, and author Dr. Ian Dunbar who brought puppy training back into fashion. By convincing people that they could and *should* teach their puppies as young as possible and making training a fun endeavor, Dr. Dunbar revolutionized the life of dogs around the world. There is no doubt in my mind that dogs everywhere say a daily group "thank you" to Dr. Dunbar. Certainly, before Dr. Dunbar's influence, there were no puppy classes and there were precious few tail wags in training.

The impact of Dr. Dunbar's fun and friendly puppy classes was overwhelming. Fun and friendly training methods worked so well with puppies that people started to use them with adolescent and adult dogs. And it worked so well with adult dogs that people tried it out with fearful and aggressive dogs too. And Bingo! It turns out friendly dog training is the method of choice for fearful or aggressive dogs. Naturally, fearsome and threatening methods are not the way to connect with fearful and threatening dogs.

As you can see by visiting a few puppy and dog training classes in your area, fun and friendly dog training has all but taken over the doggy world. Classes are filled with giggles and wagging tails; kids are involved; formal obedience competitions are getting a serious run for their money from events such as Flyball, Agility and Freestyle; and most importantly more dogs are learning how to be fun and friendly members of families.

BUILDING THE BOND

A trusting and cooperative relationship is a requirement for dog-friendly dog training. By now, you should be convinced that dog-friendly dog training is the easiest, most efficient, and most enjoyable way to go. You are now ready to move on to start achieving your training goals. The most important of which is building a trusting

Jump-Starting the Relationship

The best way to jump-start the relationship is by hand feeding your dog. This means you will get your dog's bowl off the floor and sit down and chat with him. Just as studies have shown the importance of families eating at least one meal together a day, the same is true with respect to your relationship with your dog.

So, for at least one week, set aside 5 to 10 minutes to hand feed your dog his meal. Use each piece of kibble to ask him to sit, down, stand, rollover or come. Also, practice gentling and handling exercises. Offer him a piece of kibble each time you reach out to touch a part of his body.

For each piece of kibble your dog takes from your hand, you are cementing his trust and bond with you. Consider each like a deposit in the bank that will earn you an enormous amount of "interest" over your dog's life with you.

bond between you and your dog. Actually, now that you have chosen to be a dog-friendly dog trainer you have already all but done this. You have ensured that you and your dog will be good buddies because you will be using fun and friendly techniques to teach him.

A good relationship with your dog means he will look to you for guidance. This, rather than using physical force to dominate him, is the best way to become your dog's leader. A good relationship with you is the foundation, of a great future for your dog. The more energy you focus on building this foundation the less time you will spend training. A teacher who fosters a safe and nurturing relationship with her students is most likely to help those students fulfill their full potential as quickly as possible. A child wouldn't be expected to thrive in a class with a teacher whom they feared and mistrusted, and neither can a pet dog.

Bonding with your dog couldn't be easier. Simply choose dog-friendly training methods (you've done that), and manage your dog's life so you give him the best chance to be right.

Training opens up communication channels between you and your dog. Yes! It is possible to talk to the animals.

Tools to Help
You Teach

HOW DOGS LEARN

Observing how dogs learn about their environment provides many useful clues regarding how best to teach them and which tools to use to do so. Dogs' thought is neither inferior nor superior to ours, just different. Dogs will obviously struggle with a simple math problem, but they excel when it comes to evaluating sensory input. What might fluster humans is second nature to dogs and vice versa. Because of their superior senses, the dogs' world is much more vibrant than ours. And unlike us, dogs live very much in the present. Their focus is on the here and now.

Your dog investigates everything in his universe and assesses the feedback from each stimulus—whether good, bad or innocuous. Both pleasant and unpleasant consequences strongly influence further investigatory behavior. Behaviors followed by good consequences increase in frequency and are much more likely to be repeated in the

Manipulating the rewards in your dog's life will bring you success in the training game.

future; behaviors followed by bad consequences tend to decrease in frequency and are generally less likely to occur in the future.

Dogs make thoughtful associations between their behavior and environmental cues and consequences. Moreover, dogs learn quickly by making new associations at an amazing rate. Thus, by providing appropriate feedback, owners may quickly and easily teach their dogs what they think is right and what is wrong. By manipulating the consequences of your dog's actions you can teach him to do (or not do) just about anything you want. By the same token, inappropriate feedback will teach your dog to misbehave. For example, responding to your dog when he whines will teach him that doing so is a good way to get your attention. Watch out, or before you know it your dog will be training *you* and winning the training game.

TOOLS TO HELP YOU TEACH

Tools to help you train your dog are both conceptual (methods) and concrete (things that you make or buy). And so, tools include things like taking your dog for a walk as a reward for sitting when you ask him to, or using a specific type of collar, such as a head halter.

Rewards

Rewards are the most powerful tools in training. They are the best way to say to your dog "I like what you are doing." Rewards are also the best way to keep your dog happy and interested in learning from you, and to make training fun for your dog, for you, for your family and for your friends. Rewards are at the heart of fun and friendly dog training.

Listen to the Experts

Discoveries in the fields of psychology and learning have had an incredible impact on all types of training; training employees to be more productive in the workplace, training families to communicate successfully and of course, training animals. Edward Thorndike, B. F. Skinner and many other scientists all discovered that positive reinforcement is the most powerful training tool, not punishment.

These findings were all but ignored in popular pet dog training up until about the 1980's.

By definition, a reward is anything your dog likes. It can be a kind word, a scratch behind the ear, a walk in the park, a toss of a toy, or a bit of food. The list of possible rewards is endless, but it is important to keep in mind that each dog will have unique preferences, just like us. You should have a good idea of what your dog's favorite rewards are. In fact, I recommend making a list of your dog's top 10 favorites.

Behavioral Cement

Each time you reward your dog you will make him more likely to repeat what he was doing when or just before you rewarded him. For example, give your dog a biscuit when he sits to greet you and he will be more likely to do so again. Each time you reward him for greeting you politely, you are strengthening that behavior (and weakening inappropriate greeting behaviors such as jumping up!). Also, you will strengthen your relationship with your dog because you have shown him what makes you happy, and by rewarding him you have made him happy as well.

Just as concrete reinforces the foundation of a building, rewards reinforce the foundation of your relation-ship with your dog by increasing the incidence of behaviors you like. By making good behavior stronger you are cementing the relationship between you and your dog.

Each and every reward increases your dog's eager-ness to want to do what you want him to do.

Endless Opportunities to Reward

There is an endless list of rewards for your dog, just as there is an endless list of rewards for people. It's a good thing there are so many different rewards because using dog-friendly dog training methods means there are endless opportunities to reward your dog.

Teach Your Dog to Say Please

Asking your dog to say "please" (for example, to sit), for dinner, for couch privileges, to go outside, or to play, is one of the secrets to successful pet dog training.

For example, a single trip to the beach or park is an opportunity to reward your dog many times. Take the leash in your hand and wait for your dog to sit before putting it on. Take just one step forward and wait for your dog to sit again. Continue a few steps at a time (with sits) until you get to the door. As always, before going through doors, wait for your dog to sit, then give him a piece of kibble. Go to your car (a few steps at a time) and wait for your dog to sit before opening the car door. Once at the beach, wait for your dog to sit before letting him out. Wait for your dog to sit before letting him off leash and telling him to go play. Let your dog romp around for a while and then call him back to sit for a treat. When your dog sits, tell him "go play" again and toss a ball for him. Repeat this many times as your dog investigates and plays. Every time you interrupt your dog's activities by asking him to come and sit, you can tell him to "go play" as a reward once more. By doing so, play becomes a reward, which reinforces good obedience, rather than becoming a distraction that would compete with obedience. So many rewards at your disposal during just one trip to the beach!

Don't Be Stingy!

While you should certainly vary when and what you give your dog, don't be stingy about giving rewards, especially when you are beginning to teach something new. Think of yourself as a generous (but varied) slot machine. You'll make things easier and more fun for you and your dog, and behaviors you like will be very strongly reinforced.

Turn Your Dog into a Gambler

The great thing about using rewards to train is that they are most effective when given inconsistently. This is convenient, because most of us are inconsistent!

To understand the effectiveness of inconsistent rewards, you simply need to watch a gambler in front of a slot machine. She will spend a lot of time playing the machine, even if the machine only "spits out" a few rewards. What is the glue that keeps her there? Inconsistent rewards! The gambler is hooked on playing the game because a big part of the game is the expectation of a jackpot and the thrill of not knowing when the next reward will appear.

A dog trained using dog-friendly methods is hooked on training like a gambler is hooked on gambling because you keep him guessing about when he will be rewarded and how valuable the reward will be (food, praise, a walk, or a ride in the car). In essence, you are your dog's slot machine!

Choosing Rewards

Your choice of what to use to reward will depend on personal preference and, more importantly on what works best for your dog. Make sure you know which rewards are your dog's favorites and realize this may change

Jackpot!

Randomly rewarding your dog for behaviors you like will keep him hooked on playing the training game with you. Adding in an occasional "jackpot" reward, one that's extra special, makes the game even more interesting and fun for you both. For example, when my dogs run to me especially fast when called, I make a bigger fuss than usual.

from day to day, even from minute to minute. For example, if you have been playing fetch for 10 minutes, this game might not be a high priority for your dog for a while. So, try something different.

It's a good idea to write down a list of your dog's favorite rewards ranked from 1 to 10. When you are working on new, more difficult or very important behaviors (like coming when called) you might use some of the rewards that are ranked the highest. Once your dog has learned something, you should vary the rewards as much as possible. Remember, variety is the spice of life and the secret to a well-trained dog. There is nothing worse than eating the same old lunch day after day, or watching the same movie every night. How boring! Being inventive with what and how often you offer rewards is the best way to keep your dog interested in playing the training game.

These Are a Few of My Favorite Things

Make a list of your dog's favorite rewards and reserve giving him his favorites for times when he does something really special, like coming to you quickly when you call him. My dogs' favorites are:

going for a walk

playing with other dogs

staring contests with squirrels (don't worry, they never catch them)

invites onto the bed

petting

liver treats

bread (really)

meat

squeaky toys

verbal praise

Verbal Praise

Verbal praise such as "good dog," or "who's a terrific pup?" is the first thing most people think of as a reward. This is terrific for precise timing and is especially useful because you always have your voice with you and you can use it to reward your dog from a distance!

Be sure you teach your dog that your voice means something good. Spend a week or so hand feeding your dog and tell him "good dog" before offering each piece of kibble. This way your voice will be associated with something all dogs like, food.

Attention and Affection

Spending time with your dog, hands on petting, rubbing and massaging are wonderful rewards for most dogs. This is great, because this is one of the most enjoyable aspects of living with a dog.

Attention and affection are especially good positive feedback for lengthy behaviors (such as a long down) and, of course, to teach your dog to relax and enjoy handling, examination and restraint. As a bonus, grooming, attention and affection are equally as relaxing for you, the trainer!

Be aware, attention and affection are also effective at unintentionally encouraging inappropriate and unwanted behaviors. For example, if you pet your dog when he whines or giggle when he jumps up on you, you are training him to do both. All you have to do is make sure you reserve attention and affection for times when your dog is well behaved. Some dogs may become over excited when people touch them. If your dog is like this, either reserve hands-on petting for when your dog has a good foundation of training, or use gentle, slow rhythmic petting to soothe your dog to be calm.

Toys, Activities and Games

There is a limitless number of games you can play with your dog. Active games like chasing a tennis ball, playing tug, or playing hide and seek are terrific, but so are quieter games, like a family competition to see who can get your dog to lie down quietly for the longest time for a single piece of kibble.

There also is a huge variety array of toys to choose from, including, tug toys, stuffable toys, squeaky toys and balls. To figure out which your dog likes best you can take your dog with you to the pet store and see if he shows a particular interest, or better yet, take him to visit friends with friendly dogs and see if he likes any of their toys. This is also a great way to keep up on maintaining your dog's socialization.

Rewarding your dog with affection and games is as pleasant for you as it is for your dog.

My favorite toys for dogs are the Kong toy and white sterilized bones. They are both hollow (and therefore, can be stuffed with a variety of great foods), and are all but indestructible (which means they will last a very long time). Squeaky toys are great, but I would suggest

r
s
n
r
b
c
n

only allowing your dog to play with them when you are there to supervise. These toys are easily torn apart, and there is a danger of your dog choking on some of the parts. Ropes and other tug toys are also good items to have in your reward repertoire, but they should be used for supervised play and only if you can ask your dog to let go of the toy and he does so without a fuss (later on I'll talk about teaching your dog to share). Toys are magically effective for training your dog to train himself when you are not around. For example, by stuffing a Kong with kibble, your dog will teach himself to play with his Kong and not your shoes!

Make toys a valuable reward by controlling your dog's access to them. If your dog has 10 toys lying around the house, chances are none of them will work as a very effective reward. But, if

b
s
t
t
w
e
t

you leave just a couple of stuffed chewtoys out and put the rest away, will find that when you do take them out your dog will be very interested in them. He'll also want to know what you'd like him to do in order to get them!

You can train your dog to do virtually anything when playing fetch, and it is one of the best activities to enjoy with your dog.

Remember, ask your dog to sit (or down, stand or rollover) before every privilege and pleasurable activity. For example, a ride in the car to go to the park.

The Ultimate Reward

Dogs obviously enjoy reward training. They love praise, petting, toys, treats and all the fun and games. Better yet, in no time at all, dogs come to enjoy the actual training activities. Indeed, for a reward-trained dog, the very best rewards are the actions and activities themselves.

Your dog now runs to you quickly because he likes to run to you quickly. He walks by your side because that's his favorite pastime and you are his favorite friend. Training that is built on gentle guidance, good communication and oodles of rewards, results in training itself becoming the ultimate reward. The reward lies in the training and in a sense, *the dog rewards himself.*

Once your dog has been reward trained, eventually he will require very little external reinforcement or motivation, since he enjoys playing the training game just as much as you do.

CONSEQUENCES FOR INAPPROPRIATE BEHAVIOR

Removal of Rewards (the Ultimate Punishment)

Removal of the things your dog likes best is an extremely effective way to respond to inappropriate behavior. For example, if your dog is not giving you his full attention, show him the reward he could have won, whether it be a piece of kibble, a tennis ball or a toy, and tell him "silly dog, you could have won this, but now you can't have it." Put it away, sit down and read a book. After a few minutes, try again and you will probably find your dog has better attention and an improved attitude. He will see the value in paying attention to you. This is a great opportunity to remind him that you hold the key to his "resource treasure chest."

Train your dog right, and then the best reward for walking nicely by your side is that your dog gets to walk by your side.

When you begin training your dog, keeping him on leash is the best way to get the maximum value from rewards (and their removal). This way, your dog can't just go off to look for fun elsewhere. Essentially, by controlling his access to resources, you are making yourself more valuable.

When Time Out is your best punishment, you know you have a great relationship with your dog and that you are training the right way.

Because training soon becomes one of a reward-trained dog's favorite activities, Time Out from training is the ultimate punishment. Time Out means no more training, no more rewards and no more trainer. After a short break, your dog comes back refocused on spending time with you and on the wonderful benefits of interacting with you—play, treats and toys.

During the early stages of training, either simply ignore your dog for a minute or two or you can actually leave the room. Note that when you begin training, you should make a point of always playing and training with your dog in his long-term confinement area, so that it is safe for you to immediately leave your dog alone. Better yet, have your dog on a leash so that all you have to do is stand up and ignore him.

If you have two dogs, you can ignore the inattentive dog and offer your other dog numerous rewards. Personally, I love doing this. Not only does it relieve my frustrations, but it also is the best way to get some attention.

Remember, after a Time Out, instruct your dog to come and sit to reestablish your control and to give him the opportunity to make up and to get back to playing the training game with you.

Instructive Reprimands

Many punishments do not have the desired effect because they are not instructive. It is not sufficient to just let your dog know he has

Become a Great Reward Manipulator

Focus on reinforcing your dog's behavior by manipulating rewards. This is without a doubt the best way to train. You show the dog what you want him to do and then reward him when he does it. The best way to inhibit and eliminate unwanted behavior is to train your dog to *want* to do what you want. For example, teach your dog to sit and ask him to do so when he greets you. If he is sitting, he can't be jumping on you! And if your dog does not comply, the best "punishment" is a temporary time out from training and rewards.

made a mistake. Sure, your dog knows you are upset, but what should he do to make things right? If you want your dog to learn what he should be doing, your reprimand must be instructive. "Get your KONG!" is far more effective than "NO! bad dog!" If your dog is about to eliminate indoors, the single exclamation "outside" both informs the dog he is making a mistake and lets him know where you would like him to eliminate.

Similarly, if your dog jumps up on visitors, rather than screaming "no" or "aaargh!" or "off!" simply instruct your dog to "sit."

Although screaming "no!" may startle the dog into non-activity, the dog is still not doing what you want. Anyway, it's much easier on the dog and much more effective to concentrate on telling the dog what you want him to do. This way, you are truly correcting in that you are helping your dog to be correct. Also, it's important to teach your dog that tone and volume signal urgency and emergency and not the prospect of pain or punishment. Think of how you would want your dog to react in an emergency. If he gets off leash and starts to run across a busy street, you will probably panic and yell at him. If he thinks this means he's in trouble, he may run away from you and get hurt!

Boobytraps! (Punishment Not Associated with Owner)

Boobytraps may be very effective but they are still unpleasant (by definition) and most store-bought boobytraps and alarm systems are very expensive. It much easier and much more effective to prevent your dog from misbehaving (confinement and supervision) and to teach your dog an acceptable alternative behavior. For example, providing a little occupational therapy such as a stuffed Kong in your dog's crate will work better than booby traps all over your house to stop him from chewing.

Negative Reinforcement (Not Advised)

Most people think negative reinforcement is equivalent to punishment, in reality, it's the cessation (or negation) of punishment to reinforce appropriate behavior. Although it may be an effective training technique, it's often necessary to punish the dog for very long periods of time before the dog behaves as desired. This of course, is extremely unpleasant and puts you on thin ice regarding your dog's temperament. Indeed, many dogs "crack" when negative reinforcement is ill-applied.

Non-Instructive Reprimand (Definitely Not Advised)

Continually harping after your dog "No! bad dog!" with a high volume, nasty tone and ugly face just tells the dog that you don't like him. But you do like your dog, it is merely his behavior which you consider to be unacceptable. Many owners lose it when reprimanding their dogs. They end up yelling emotionally. Being yelled at is stressful. Like people, dogs have a hard time learning when under stress. Why are you yelling? Your dog is not deaf! And if he is deaf, he can't hear you! So, please, stop yelling.

Physical Punishments from Owner (Definitely, Absolutely Not Advised)

This is how you want to treat your best friend? More disturbingly, physical punishment is almost always non-instructive—the dog has no idea why he is being abused. Harsh physical punishments are totally inappropriate, un-called for and utterly unacceptable in pet dog training.

Side Effects of Punishment

Focusing on punishing your dog is relatively ineffective and has a number of serious side effects on the dog's temperament and on your relationship. Even when punishment training has been apparently effective in resolving simple behavior problems, it invariably shakes the dog's confidence and undermines the trusting relationship between trainer and dog, which will ultimately destroy the dog's temperament. Punishments that are administered by the owner become quickly associated with both the owner and the training process. The result—the dog may learn to comply, grudgingly, but he has also begun to learn to dislike training, and the trainer.

For example, when a dog has been punished for jumping up, he may not jump up anymore but he probably likes the owner just a little bit less. The trainer has won the battle but lost the war. The dog may become progressively more fearful with each punishment. If ever the dog expresses his dislike for training, the "stubborn" dog will be punished all the more severely. And if ever the dog decides to correct the trainer for a poor choice in training techniques, the poor dog will of course receive the death penalty.

One of the most common problems associated with punishment based techniques is that many pet dogs quickly become desensitized to corrections, causing the owner to go from light corrections to stronger and stronger corrections. Gentle tugs on a buckle collar become firmer jerks on a metal choke collar, which are then disbanded for even firmer yanks on a spiked metal "pinch" collar or zaps from an electroic shock collar. The poor dogs suffer all because their owners did not

Yelling at your dog really only teaches him that you are enjoying train-ing as little as he is. Why not just calmly show him what you would like him to do and reward him for doing so?

No-No's

Rather than yelling "no" at your dog when he does something you don't like, why not give him a little constructive criticism? For example, if he is jumping, tell him to sit.

fully understand a technique, which at its best is severely flawed. Because dogs are social animals, they are often only too willing to put up with many high level punishments if only to be allowed to stay as part of a social group. Higher tech pain-delivery equipment is not the solution to the problems we have with our dogs.

Finally, using punishment-based techniques is the best way to create owner absent behavior problems. Your dog will wait until you leave to do things because then you, "the punisher," are not there to punish. Think about when you are exceeding the speed limit. If you see a police car, you slow down, but you'll continue to speed if you think that you can get away with it. The same applies to your dog. If you punish him when you are there, he'll learn to behave in certain ways when you are not there. Your dog is not misbehaving out of spite, he's simply acting like a dog at times when he feels that it's safe to do so.

And punishment is time-consuming. You have to be present to punish your dog. Most people cannot and do not want to stay home all day so they can constantly reprimand their dog. As a result, punishment is administered after the dog has already misbehaved, allowing the dog to destroy the living room before training is even half way completed. In real life however, after just one or two punishments, no doubt the dog would become a closet chewer, reserving his chewing activities for times when his owner is away. Even if the exercise were possible, one hundred punishment training sessions is a lot of work. Why not just train the dog to chew one chewtoy?

It can not be overemphasized that the main focus of pet dog training is teaching dogs what we think is right, not punishing them for what we think is wrong. Without a doubt this is the easiest, most efficient, most effective and indeed the most enjoyable way to teach your dog.

THE REWARD/REPRIMAND RAINBOW

Removal of Rewards

Instructive Reprimands

Booby Traps

Negative Reinforcement

Non-Instructive
Reprimands

Physical Punishment

Don't make your dog blue.

Verbal Praise

Attention and Affection

Toys, Activities and Games

Treats

Life Rewards

Internal Motivation

Focus on rewarding your dog
for getting it right.

TOOLS TO BUY

There are lots of tools to help you train your dog. In fact, there are so many that it can be quite confusing! Really though, there are only a few basics that you will need.

Collars

Your dog needs a buckle collar. It is essential for safety. Your dog must always have identification and ID tags can be conveniently attached to the buckle collar. Similarly, collars offer a convenient attachment for your leash, so your dog can safely be walked on the sidewalk and trained in open areas.

I would recommend a cheap buckle collar for puppies, because they will outgrow them quickly. You can buy your dog a special leather or nylon collar when he is full-grown.

Head Halters

Head halters are a wonderful, humane alternative to pain-inducing collars. Halters afford the owner considerable mechanical advantage to manage overly strong, active and otherwise out of control dogs.

Head halters work on the age-old horsey premise that it is easier to lead an animal by its nose than by its neck. There are a variety of halters on the market, each with it's own innovations. Used correctly,

Looks Can Be Deceiving

Unfortunately, halter-type collars are sometimes mistaken for muzzles, creating an image problem for these handy tools. But don't let their looks bother you. They work like a dream!

these halters offer almost instantaneous control of rambunctious or untrained dogs. At first your dog might find this collar to feel a bit strange (much in the same ways that puppies react when first fitted with a buckle collar). To make this adjustment as easy as possible, simply spend one or two meals hand-feeding your dog his kibble as you put the halter on and take it off. Then, stand up and entice your dog to walk with you by luring him with a piece of his kibble. Walk smoothly, without jerking on the leash or stopping, and frequently reward your dog for walking with you. Before you know it, your dog will be happy to have the halter on, because it signals the beginning of a delightful walk (which you will do more of now that your dog is so much easier to control).

Head halters are the physical equivalent of luring a dog with a food treat, lead him by his nose and the rest will follow.

Would you ever try to jerk a bear around?

Leashes

There are two basic options in the leash department, a standard 3- to 6-foot nylon or leather leash or an expandable leash. I strongly recommend using a standard leash until your dog has learned to walk nicely by your side. An expandable or retractable leash is wonderful for allowing a dog a wider area to roam, but nothing encourages a dog to pull more than allowing constant tension in the leash.

The Leash Gets a Bum Rap

Leash training has gained a bad reputation because so many people associate leashes with collar corrections and punishments. This is too bad, because some aspects are extremely beneficial.

The greatest benefit of leash training is safety. A leashed dog can safely be trained on the street, which of course is convenient because you certainly want to be able to take your dog for walks on the street. Leash training also facilitates adult dog-training classes. The leash offers control and safety, which may be easily incorporated into reward training methods.

The leash is a wonderful training tool to help your dog settle down and to walk calmly on leash. Simply tie the leash to an immovable object and your dog will soon settle down. Even better, tie both your dog's leash and a food-stuffed Kong to an eye-hook in the baseboard next to his bed. Before you know it your dog will learn to settle down quietly on his bed and chew his chewtoy.

For the leash to be effective it doesn't have to be used punitively. It can be like holding a child's hand for gentle guidance. When walking a child on a busy city street you hold his hand for safety. You don't hold hands to hurt or cause pain. Think of a leash in the same way—a convenient means to hold your dog's "hand."

Simply focus on using the leash passively (to gently guide and stop behaviors) rather than actively (to jerk your dog around). Use the leash but do not abuse the leash. Use it for safety and for occasional motivational prompting but don't use it to cause pain or administer harsh punishment.

And remember: No matter how well trained you think your dog is, keep him on leash unless surrounded by walls or fences.

The 4 C's of Leash Safety

1. Common Sense   3. Courtesy to Others
2. Control   4. Catastrophe Prevention

Crate

There are two basic kinds of crates; plastic and metal. I tend to prefer the plastic, if only for the fact that it can be used to transport your dog by air, if need be.

A plastic crate is one of the most useful tools for just about every aspect of training. It is a valuable aid for housetraining, chewtoy training, teaching your dog to calmly accept time alone, and it can also be wonderful when you travel with your pet.

The crate should be sized appropriately for your dog. It should be just large enough for your dog to stand up, turn around and lay down in. Keep in mind that if you buy a crate for your young puppy, you will need to get a larger size as he grows up. A cost-efficient solution is to buy a large crate and block off part of it until your puppy "grows into it."

Bear in mind that the crate is a temporary tool. Your dog may have full run of the house once he understands the rules, but you'll probably find your dog will still choose to go to his crate when he needs peace and quiet.

Chewtoys

Every dog should have at least four hollow, stuffable chewtoys. The best are Kongs and white sterilized bones. Rotate giving your dog two freshly stuffed toys each day. When you are home and can supervise your dog, he can chew by your side or on his blanket. If you have to leave, be sure to let him settle comfortably in his confinement area with a few good chewtoys.

Creating a chewtoy habit in your dog may save you and your dog more grief and aggravation than you can possibly imagine. The list of "wrong" things that your dog can do to keep himself occupied (both when you are home and especially when you are away), is endless. However, if you made a list of the "right" things your pet dog can do in your home, it would be pretty short, especially if it included activities for when you weren't home. Teaching your dog to do one "right"

Confining a dog to a crate with a stuffed chewtoy is like confining a child to his room with a video game, or a good book!

thing is obviously much easier and less time consuming than teaching him not to do an endless list of wrongs.

Even the smallest dog can do a lot of damage to a home in a very short period of time. Damage done by chewing alone can be immense. But you can't expect to stop your dog from chewing altogether. After all, it is one of the few pet dog hobbies. All you have to do is teach your dog *what* to chew. The quickest and easiest prevention and solution to these many potential problems is to make your dog a chewtoy junkie!

Most dogs will immediately become engrossed in a stuffed toy, especially if you are a "creative stuffer." Try lots of different fillings to

Chewtoys?

Or total household destruction?

find which ones your dog likes best. Let your dog watch you as you stuff the toys with some special fillings (peanut butter, cream cheese, and cold cuts are my dog's favorites). Use just a small bit of filling and make it tough for your dog to get at. Your dog will spend his day enjoyably engrossed in the task of trying to get to the center of his chewtoys.

Paws to Consider

Your dog's crate and chewtoys are most effective when used together. Put a stuffed bone or Kong in your dog's crate before you leave and close the crate door with your dog out of the crate. This way he will become occupied with getting in to it, not with your imminent departure. The old saying, "you always want what you can't have" is at play here. When you open the door a minute or two later, chances are he will dive right in.

If you catch your dog in the act of chewing an inappropriate article do not resort to yelling at him. Reprimanding him is the quickest way to develop an owner absent chewing problem. He will learn to wait until you are gone to chew. Ultimately, you want him not to chew inappropriate items regardless of your presence. Think about supervising him when you're home and confining him to his area with some good chewtoys when you can't keep your eye on him.

Given the lack of "Working Retriever Wanted" ads in the employment section of your local paper, don't be surprised if any and every item that is not nailed to the wall ends up being carried around in your dog's mouth. Play fetch with appropriate objects (toys). Then, your dog will know that only certain things are meant to be played with.

Don't give your puppy or dog any items to chew on that resemble items you don't want him to chew on. A dog cannot distinguish your worn-out tennis shoes from a brand new pair. And don't give your dog real bones that have been cooked. Once cooked, the bones soften and can easily splinter. Bone splinters can injure your dog's mouth and his stomach.

Special Puppy Chewtoy Considerations

Between the ages of 3 to 6 months your puppy will be losing his baby teeth as his adult teeth grow in, this is called teething. During this time, your puppy will experience discomfort and chewing will help to

Let Your Dog Act a Little Wild

In the wild, dogs spend 80 percent of their waking hours searching for food. But, we put the same food in the same bowl in the same place every day for our dogs. Make life a little more fun for your dog, hide his dinner in a Kong toy, or better yet in a few different Kongs, and give your dog a chance to act like a dog again.

alleviate it. Make sure your puppy always has an appropriate chewtoy available, especially during this teething period. Some puppies like to chew on ice cubes.

TOOLS YOU WON'T NEED

Devices designed to cause discomfort and pain exist because people believe that high-tech equipment is the cure-all for our dogs' problems. But most expensive gadgets don't offer a magic remedy. In reality, a better understanding of reward training is the answer. Resorting to extreme physical measures to train dogs just advertises that the trainer has neither really understood, nor applied, the much more effective reward training techniques.

Even when used correctly, painful punishment tools have significant side effects. Moreover, when misused by the general public, the side effects are often disastrous on the relationship between dog and owner. Work on training your dog in a friendly way instead.

Housetraining

ousetraining can be a breeze with dog-friendly methods. Teach your dog what is right (there is only one right place to go), manage the problem (when not supervised keep your dog confined to prevent mistakes) and use gentle methods to reward your dog for doing the right thing in the right place at the right time.

BECOME A GOOD DOGGY TIME MANAGER

Being a good "doggy time manager" is really what housetraining is all about—making sure that your dog is in the right place at the right time. Mistakes happen because either the dog is in the right place at the wrong time or the wrong place at the right time. If, for example, you take your dog for a walk to relieve himself when he doesn't need to go, he will probably need to go when he gets back inside!

Every time your puppy gets it right, getting it right is reinforced. So set your pup up to get it right!

During housetraining your dog needs to be taken to his doggy toilet (the right place) when he needs to eliminate (the right time), and he needs to be rewarded for going. All you have to do is make sure you don't give him the opportunity to make any mistakes in the wrong spot, and pretty soon your dog will have developed a strong habit and desire to eliminate in a particular area (his doggy toilet). Developing this strong habit is the essence of housetraining.

Dogs usually need a trip to the doggy toilet after a meal, so a well-planned feeding and watering schedule will help you to determine when your dog will need to relieve himself. Your dog will also need to go after playing and when he wakes up. So, you can pretty sure that your dog will need to go to the bathroom when he wakes up, soon after eating and drinking, and after playing.

However, successful housetraining requires more accurate prediction of when your dog needs to go and the best way to do so is by using confinement. Confining your dog to a small area, such as a crate, inhibits your dog from eliminating because puppies and dogs naturally want to keep their sleeping area clean. And so, your dog will need to eliminate when you release him from his crate and take him to his doggy toilet.

Don't fall into the trap that confining your dog is cruel. Using confinement in an educated manner is not unkind, especially considering how it accelerates housetraining (and chewtoy training) and therefore, how quickly your dog can be trusted to spend his time in all safe areas of your home.

When Should Housetraining Start?

Consider how important first impressions are with people. Well, they are just as important for your new dog or puppy. What you allow your new companion to do for the first few days in his home will set the precedent for a lifetime. You should begin housetraining the very first day you bring home your new puppy or adult dog. In fact, the very first thing you should do is take your dog to his doggy toilet to relieve himself. If you allow him to go into the house with a full bladder and/or bowel, he may make a mistake in the house, and this will set the precedent for years to come. So, the sooner you start showing him where his doggy toilet is, the better.

TOOLS FOR TIME MANAGEMENT

Long-term confinement, short-term confinement, and supervision are the three best tools to aid you in housetraining. The wise use of all three will help your dog to avoid mistakes whether you are home or not. As a side benefit, confinement is a great way to prevent separation anxiety and both confinement and supervision are great ways to avoid inappropriate chewing.

Long-term Confinement

If your schedule does not permit you to be there to allow your puppy or "adult dog in housetraining" out for frequent opportunities to eliminate, then you should leave him in a long-term confinement area.

This area should provide your dog with everything he will need—a bed, chewtoys, water, and a suitable indoor toilet. The indoor toilet is only necessary until your puppy has built sufficient bladder and bowel control and can be expected to "hold it" for several hours at a time. However, if you have a very small dog, you may choose to have your dog use an indoor toilet permanently.

If you leave an unhousetrained dog confined to a crate for a long period of time, he will be forced to soil his sleeping area. This is not only unkind, but it will also make it extremely difficult to housetrain him. So, for lengthy periods of confinement, leave your dog in an area that has a toilet.

When spending time in his long-term confinement area, your dog can't make housesoiling (and chewing) mistakes in the rest of the house. So, rather than leaving your puppy or dog to roam around your home and make mistakes (which he will inevitably be punished for later), it is much wiser to simply keep your dog in one safe area.

Yippee!!! You're Here!

When you go to get your puppy from his area in the morning ,don't encourage his excitement at your arrival. This will only make him more likely to have an accident before you get him to his toilet. Instead, calmly walk in and immediately pick him up to bring him to the area where he is expected to relieve himself. Then, of course, let him know how fantastic it is that he went in the right place.

An ideal and easy-to-construct long-term confinement area.

Long-term confinement options:

◆ A bathroom gated off with a baby gate

◆ An exercise pen

◆ An exercise pen including a crate. In this case, the crate is the dog's bedroom, and the dog's toilet is in the area sectioned off by the ex-pen.

◆ A crate connected to a doggy door that leads to a safely enclosed dog run. Your dog will essentially have a toilet and bedroom. With this setup, your dog will all but housetrain himself!

Short-term Confinement

The primary function of short-term confinement is to predict the time of elimination. Your dog has a natural inhibition against soiling

What's a Tie Down?

A tie down is sort of like a crate without walls. Using a leash, tie your dog to a stable object (a heavy piece of furniture or an eye-hook in the wall), or simply step on the leash to keep your dog at your side. Just as with a crate, a tie down is meant to inhibit your dog's elimination and to keep him in a safe area so he can't chew inappropriate objects.

Supervision

Just as you would diligently supervise a young child in your home, so should you diligently supervise a puppy or "adult dog in housetraining." Until he is housetrained, any time your dog spends in the home (outside of the two confinement areas) should be supervised. This means you must be able to give him 100% of your attention. Taking your eyes off your dog for even a few moments is plenty of time for him to urinate, defecate or chew on the furniture.

Some owners prefer a simple tie down, "a crate without walls."

It is a great idea to keep your puppy or new adult dog on leash during these supervised times out of his confinement areas until he is housetrained and chewtoy-trained. The leash will remind you to watch him like a hawk. It is also a good idea to only bring him into areas of the home outside of his confinement area when you know he has any empty bladder and bowel (only after you have just seen him eliminate in his doggy toilet), or until he is housetrained.

For the first week, have the leash connected to you. Either step on it to keep your dog by your side, hold it in your hand or tie a longer leash around your waist. Your pup can spend this time playing a game with you, chewing on a chewtoy at your side or just resting.

As your puppy or dog starts to understand the rules you can give him a little more access to the room you are in by letting him drag the leash behind him. Eventually, he will be housetrained and chewtoy-trained and will be able to enjoy time off leash in the home.

Give your dog a chewtoy, step on his leash and settle down with a good book. Within no time your dog will have a habit of settling quietly at your side, even without a leash on. Every hour, take him to his doggy toilet and let him relieve himself.

CHOOSING A DOGGY TOILET

One of the first things you need to do is choose where you want your dog to eliminate. There are three basic options for your dog's toilet: Outside on grass or concrete, inside on a doggy toilet, or both inside and outside. Having an adult dog who is trained to go inside on a doggy toilet can be very convenient and is often the choice for small dogs.

Housetraining Puppies Versus Adult Dogs

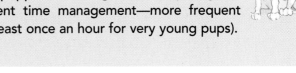

The only difference between housetraining a puppy and an adult is time. Pups take a little longer because of their limited bladder and bowel capacity. Consequently, puppies need to go more frequently and therefore require more diligent time management—more frequent trips to their doggy toilet (at least once an hour for very young pups).

Indoor Potty Training

If you have a very young puppy and your veterinarian has advised you not to take the pup outside until he has all his shots, then use a temporary indoor toilet. This is also a good idea because a very young puppy needs to go to the bathroom so often (just like a human baby) that it is inconvenient for most people to have to take him outside often enough (especially if you live in a high-rise apartment). If your schedule permits, you can avoid using an indoor toilet as long as you have a safe outdoor area to take your young puppy (a fenced yard).

Paper-training

If you choose to paper-train your pup, cover the entire floor with paper so he can't make mistakes off of it. Don't assume that your pup will know to target a small area of paper. Every few days, remove a sheet or two until you are down to a small covered area. If he misses the paper, then you have taken up too much too fast and you should go back and cover more of the floor with it. Obviously, you will want to replace the paper several times a day, so stock up!

A Smooth Transition

It is a good idea to have an indoor doggy toilet that has the same surface as the one he will eventually use outside. Most people try to housetrain young puppies by first teaching them to go on paper and then outside on grass or concrete. But switching surfaces (from paper to grass or concrete) when the dog is three to four months old means housetraining is a two-step process. First, teaching the dog to go on one surface inside and then another outside. If you intend for your adult dog to have an outside toilet, bring a little bit of the great outdoors into your home. Get a roll of grass turf or a thin slab of concrete and place it in a large plastic litter box or car oil drip pan. If you choose to use grass turf or concrete in a litter pan, simply confine your pup to an area that is small enough that the pan takes up most of the area (aside from his bed). This arrangement may sound a little strange, but it will make housetraining all the easier.

You will need to replace the grass or concrete at least once a week. Unless you want your dog to be litter-box trained in the future, you will only use this indoor doggy toilet until the puppy is old enough to go outside and control his bladder and bowels for longer periods of time.

If you must use a temporary indoor toilet, be sure to use every opportunity (evenings and weekends) to get your pup to the right spot outside so you can make an easier transition to getting him to go outside.

Quick Tips for Housetraining

- Give your dog every opportunity he needs to eliminate in the place you have chosen as his toilet.
- Give your dog zero opportunity to eliminate anywhere else.
- Praise and reward him lavishly when he goes on his doggy toilet.

OUTDOOR TRAINING

When you take your dog out to his doggy toilet, stand in one area and wait for him to go. Don't make the mistake of trying to walk your dog around the block to get him to go. Usually, this prolongs the process because your dog will get distracted, and some dogs who like to walk learn to "hold it" because they learn the walk ends the moment they

A roll of turf is a marvelous innovation for a temporary indoor doggy toilet, (this will speed up housetraining like you can't believe).

"go." Instead, teach your dog to go to the bathroom right when you take him outside to a designated spot. Then the walk can be a reward for prompt elimination. On a cold and rainy night, you will be glad you taught your dog to go quickly!

If your dog doesn't go within 5 minutes, go back inside, keep your dog on a leash at your side, sit down and read or watch television for about 20 minutes before going back out to try again.

Perfect Aim

If you don't want your dog to use the whole yard as a toilet, you can train him to relieve himself in a specific area. Dogs are very particular about where they eliminate, but it is very easy to teach your dog to go in a specific spot. Use posts and or string to create a boundary. Take your dog on leash to this spot and reward him with a special treat. In no time, he'll head straight for his special spot as you go out the door.

HOUSE-SOILING MISTAKES

How to Get Your Dog Back on Track

If your adult dog is soiling in the house, the first thing to do is to visit your veterinarian to make sure the problem is not caused by a medical condition. If she says everything is A-OK, then there are just a few steps to getting your dog back on the right housetraining track. Be sure to confine him to a long-term confinement area when you can't supervise him, and give him three liver treats when he goes in the right spot. In no time flat, you'll have a dog who sees the value in going in the right place.

Keep Your Cool

Accidents happen no matter how diligent you are. Whatever you do, don't get angry at your dog. If your dog makes a mistake in the house, yelling at him or otherwise punishing him will serve only to teach him two things: that you aren't so nice after all and that you don't like to see him go to the bathroom. Your dog will think "obviously my owner has some weird urination issues and wants me to do it in private."

As a result, he will learn that the safest time to eliminate is when you aren't around, and you will find he is highly unlikely to go when you are at the other end of the leash. Instead he will find hidden spots, like behind the couch. Remember, if your dog makes a mistake

Housetraining is as easy as 1,2,3: 1. Confine your dog to prevent all mistakes and 2. to predict when he needs to go, so that . . . 3. you can take your dog to the right place and handsomely reward him!

in the house, it tells you he isn't housetrained after all. Either you failed to put him in the right place when he needed to go or to confine him when you couldn't watch him.

If You Catch Him in the Act

If your dog eliminates in front of you in the house, quickly say "outside." Then quickly scoop him up and take him to his doggy toilet. Praise him when he goes out there.

Submissive Urination

If your dog urinates when he greets you or others, or when you yell at him, he is letting you know that you are the boss. Submissive urination is most frequently seen in dogs that lack confidence due to inadequate socialization and in dogs that have been the subject of physical or verbal corrections.

Immediately discontinue using any sort of punishments; they will only make matters worse. Your dog is urinating as an appeasement gesture. If you respond with a correction, your dog is likely to get even more nervous and urinate more. Furthermore, you will be further damaging your relationship with your dog.

The solution is to practice nicely asking your dog to sit to greet you. Reward him with calm praise and a bit of a treat. Repeat greetings

After being yelled at for going in the house, this dog is thinking that his owner has some urination hang-ups.

As a result, he has learned not to go when the neurotic one is watching.

And so he is forced to hide to eliminate.

several times. If he urinates on the first greeting, simply ignore him. Leave, come back and greet him again. It is unlikely he will urinate on the second or subsequent greetings, and so you may reward him for dry greetings.

Don't yell at or hit your dog if he makes a mistake in the house; it will only make matters worse. Instead, reprimand yourself!

You should also work on socializing this dog to lots of people so that he has a boost in self-confidence. You might consider taking him to a dog-training class or dog park where he is sure to meet lots of dog-friendly people, or invite some friends over.

THE THREE STEPS TO SUCCESSFUL HOUSETRAINING

Remember, housetraining is really a question of time management.

1. Make sure your dog is never in the wrong place at the right time. This ensures that your dog doesn't make any mistakes because each mistake sets the precedent for more to follow.

2. Make sure your dog is in the right place at the right time, when he needs to go to the bathroom.

3. And the real secret of successful housetraining is predicting when your dog needs to go, so that you may take your dog to his doggy toilet at the appropriate time and reward him for going.

Improve Your Dog's Social Life

can't think of a more important quality in a pet dog than to be friendly to people, especially children. Consequently, there is no more pressing item on your dog's training agenda than socialization. Socialization makes your dog fit to be a great companion. Well-socialized dogs develop more confidence and do not become overly dependent on their owners. They are better equipped to calmly handle a variety of situations around people or when left at home alone. Because friendly dogs are a pleasure to be around, owners enjoy spending time playing with and training them. In turn, the dogs are much less likely to chew or bark excessively or soil in the house. Obviously a well-socialized dog has no need to hide or bite. And certainly well-socialized dogs are more likely to live longer, happier and healthier lives.

WHAT IS SOCIALIZATION?

Socialization is the process that makes your dog friendly with animals and, most importantly, with people. Sure, it would be a severe

The Benefits of Good Social Skills

A well-socialized dog is a friend to all, and he'll be a welcome guest. Yes, you want your dog to be a party animal! Most behavior problems including aggression, fear, housesoiling, not coming when called, separation anxiety, chewing and barking stem from poor socialization. Easy decision, no?

inconvenience if your dog were unfriendly with other dogs (especially if you must walk your dog on the street and pass other dogs). But it would be a constant worry if your dog were unfriendly to people, and it would be a disaster if your dog were not friendly to family members.

Socializing the dog to the family is the first step, but this alone is not sufficient. Many owners of super-friendly family dogs have a rude awakening when their dog snaps at a child, stranger or veterinarian. It's great that the dog likes Mom, Dad, the two kids and a couple of family friends, since these are the people your dog will spend most of his time with. But, socialization means teaching your dog to be friendly and accepting of *all* people you introduce him to, especially unfamiliar children and men. It is not sufficient to teach your dog just to get along with his usual social circle. There is always the chance that an unfamiliar child or veterinary nurse will handle your dog, and you want him to be prepared for the encounter.

Be aware that socialization is an ongoing process. Your dog must continue to meet unfamiliar people (and animals) throughout his life if you wish for him to continue to be a friendly dog.

*Take your dog for frequent trips down
the socialization roadway.*

PUPPY SOCIALIZATION

Although you can obedience train a dog at any age, a sound temperament is something that must be developed early in life. If you delay this process, you can still socialize your adolescent or adult dog, but it will be much more time consuming and you will be playing catch up for years to come.

Watchdogs Are Friendly Too!

A lot of people are resistant to socializing their dog to strangers because they want their dog to be protective. Your dog's innate ability to choose between friend and foe might be pretty accurate, but eventually he will make a mistake. It's much smarter to first socialize your dog so he is confident and secure in the company of all people. Then, if you choose, train your dog to bark or growl on cue as a protective ruse.

The concept of early socialization and puppy training was rediscovered and popularized by dogs' best friend, English veterinarian and behaviorist Dr. Ian Dunbar. No other single training innovation has had such a dramatic influence on the lives of pet dogs and their owners worldwide than this one. Early socialization is the best way to create your perfect companion and to avoid behavior and temperament problems.

Certainly, puppy training concepts are not new. In fact they're so old they're new again! Both dog and horse texts from the 1800s talk about early training and gentling procedures, but many of these concepts were lost to the world of dog and horse trainers for the greater part of the 20th century. However, the word has spread, and puppy socialization and training deadlines are at the forefront of modern dog lovers' agendas.

Getting Used to Sounds

It is vital that very young pups are exposed to a variety of noises, especially during the first few weeks of life as their ears are opening. This enables developing pups to become accustomed to loud and potentially scary noises in a gradual fashion.

Perhaps the most important precaution an owner can take is to ensure that their new puppy has been raised indoors. Not in a barn, not in a kennel, but indoors in the kitchen or living room so that he is in the center of all of the action. This precaution is especially important with the sound-sensitive breeds (all the good obedience and guarding breeds). If you have done your homework and chosen a pup who has been raised inside a home, then you know he is already off to a good start on his journey down the socialization highway! But don't fret if you are adopting a puppy and don't know his background. Simply do your best to expose him to a host of normal, everyday noises in his new home. So, no tiptoeing around this little guy. Turn up the radio, open the windows and start vacuuming!

Make Your Dog a Social Climber

Climbing the social ladder can be tough for people, but you can have a whole lot of fun helping your dog climb his social ladder. Let him experience as many things as possible in a rewarding setting so that he becomes a confident and well-adjusted member of your family. The earlier you start the better. By 16 weeks, your puppy's view of the world and his place in it has already become well established, but it is never too late for your dog to become better socially equipped.

Socialization Checklist: Getting Used to Sounds

Television

Vacuum cleaner

People knocking at the door

Storms

Children playing (shouting and screaming)

Radio

Traffic

Getting Comfortable with Being Handled

Teaching your dog to willingly, and happily, accept handling is a crucial aspect of socialization. Don't wait until your dog cuts his foot to find out that he doesn't

FX's Pet Department is wonderful to socialize your puppy to sounds on the TV!

like his feet touched. Practice handling exercises so your dog will be comfortable with having all parts of his body being handled.

Of course, the best time to practice is when hand-feeding your puppy or dog his dinner. Set aside 5 or 10 minutes every day to "play vet" with your puppy. Sit down in a quiet area of your home with a few pieces of your puppy's kibble. Have your puppy on a leash and start by gently touching his head for one second while you give him a piece of kibble. Then touch his mouth for one second and give him a piece of kibble. Continue until you have touched all over his body and used up all of his kibble. Next time, touch each spot for two seconds and then three.

Don't forget to gently examine his mouth, take a look inside his ears and check out what's going on between his little toes. For each new area you touch, offer him a tasty bit of kibble. Be especially generous when you touch areas that your pup is more sensitive about.

At least once a day, invite your dog over for a belly rub. This is a great way to show him how enjoyable a subordinate gesture can be.

Dinnertime Handling

Don't just put your dog's food down and walk away. Hang around while he is eating. Touch him and talk to him. Every once in a while (particularly when you touch him) put a tasty treat in his bowl to show him how rewarding it is to have humans around his bowl.

A tummy rub and a treat will teach any puppy to love handling.

Socialization Checklist: Getting Used to Handling

Touch your puppy's head

Touch your puppy's collar.

Touch your puppy's back.

Touch your puppy's tummy.

Touch your puppy's paws.

Touch your puppy's rear end.

Look inside your puppy's ears.

Look inside your puppy's mouth.

You Look Marvelous!

No matter what type of coat your dog has, he should be comfortable letting you groom him. Even if it is just to wipe his body with a towel, clip his nails and clean his ears. If you set aside five minutes a day for a couple of weeks, you'll find that you will have a dog who loves to be groomed.

Have your dog on leash and tie him to something stable. Get his dinner and a few extra treats in a bowl and sit next to him. Start with one stroke of the brush, and then offer a piece of food. Now try two strokes and then a piece of food. Move on to picking up one foot and laying the clippers against his foot, and offer a bit of food. Then, look into one of his ears and offer a piece of food. Don't rush things. Take time to make sure your puppy enjoys minimal examining before you move on to actually clipping a nail or cleaning his ears.

Getting to Know People

In order to keep up with his developmental timetable (see *Dog Behavior: An Owner's Guide to a Happy Healthy Pet*, published by Howell Book House), your puppy needs to be well on his way to being thoroughly socialized to people by the time he is three months old. As a rule of thumb, your pup needs to meet 50 different people in a positive setting. Fifty people? And the puppy is still too young to

Gotcha!

In an emergency, you may need to grab your dog to get a hold of him, and it could result in a tragedy if your dog doesn't allow you to do so. Teach your dog to accept being grabbed by teaching him that it is a rewarding experience. Many times throughout the day reach down to grab your dog's collar and at the same time give him a treat. In no time at all your dog is going to love being grabbed.

venture on the streets? Actually, it's easy. All you have to do is invite people to your home and have a few puppy parties!

I've had many people tell me that this is an unrealistic demand to make of a new puppy owner. But, again, there is absolutely nothing that's more important for a pet dog than to be well socialized and friendly. And there is no time better to do this than in early puppyhood. Investing time and energy into this process early on will save you a whole lot of time, energy (and probably grief) later on. Anyway, socializing your puppy is fun!

Puppy Parties

If you want to produce a dog who is friendly with people and other animals, you must begin socializing in puppyhood and maintain socialization throughout your dog's life. In order to do this, your dog has to meet numerous people in a pleasant and rewarding setting.

There is no better way to do this than to have numerous puppy parties in your home.

Initially, invite close family and friends, and teach them all to use kibble to teach your dog to come and sit and lie down. Not only will your friends train your dog for you but your dog will learn to love them. Next, invite groups of women, then men (offer pizza), then children (have games ready to play), a few at a time.

Once the puppy is thoroughly at ease with all sorts of people, it's time for a little frivolity. Have costume parties where everybody wears a hat, carries something unusual and adopts all sorts of silly mannerisms. All the time, have people use your puppy's dinner kibble to train him to come, sit and lie down. This might sound a little ridiculous, but it's for a serious reason. Basically, after a series of puppy parties like these, there is nothing in the real world that will really scare your dog. For example, if a child

Puppy parties are the best way to improve your dog's social life, and yours too!

dressed up for Halloween as a green frog "hops" by your dog and taps him on the head with a wand, your pup will say "been there, done that" and wag his tail happily.

Get your dog used to the strange things people do, like staring and manhandling. Sadly, not everyone is respectful of a dog's limits, and it's likely that at some point someone will touch your dog a little more roughly than is appropriate. So, get your dog used to this now when he is a puppy. In fact, if you do things right you will have a dog who not only tolerates, but *enjoys* just about any sort of handling!

Start by having family members hand feed while they stare at and touch the pup. Start off touching him very gently. Gradually, increase the force of your handling. At the same time you might want to increase the rewards. This only means that you should work up to being able to being as rough as a typical child might be if he were unsupervised. After practicing things for a week or so, invite a friend over and have her hand feed your dog while she gently touches him and you handle him a little more roughly. Eventually, you should have a dog who is comfortable with just about anyone handling him in just about any way (within reason of course).

As a note of caution, it is important to maintain routine hygiene at all times. So, make sure household guests wash their hands and take off their shoes before playing with your puppy.

Socialization Checklist: Getting to Know People

Family	People who move slowly
Friends	People who move quickly
Visitors (strangers)	People at your house
Children	People in the street
Men	People in the park
People wearing hats	People in wheelchairs
People carrying things (canes, baseball bats, bags, umbrellas)	

Getting to Know Animals

Most of the socialization to animals will have to wait until the pup is over three months old and has completed his series of puppy shots. In fact, since the pup has been in virtual social isolation (at least as to dogs) for the last month, socializing your puppy to dogs now becomes a major priority. Enroll your dog in puppy class right away and make sure you are walking your dog at least once a day so he can meet lots of dogs on the street. Remember, although it's important, it's not sufficient that your dog becomes friendly with a small circle of canine friends. He must learn how to greet unfamiliar dogs as well. And so a good tip is to walk a different route each day in addition to going to your dog's familiar dog park.

Playing with another dog can be great exercise (both mentally and physically) for your dog. Look for a dog run in your area, or set up doggy play dates with people from dog training class. You can also use this time to practice having your dog greet people nicely by sitting.

If you want to socialize your puppy to the resident household cat, you have already done the right thing by starting off early. It is much easier for an adult cat and a young puppy to work things out than an adult dog and a young kitten. Depending on where you live, you may or may not want to socialize your dog to horses and livestock and to teach him not to chase or otherwise harass livestock or wild animals. Simply keep him on leash to prevent problems, and teach him to pay attention to you when you ask him to sit, down and come when called (even around other animals).

Socialization Checklist: Getting to Know Animals

Dogs of all ages	Horses
Cats	Livestock
Pocket pets (Hamsters, Rabbits, Rats)	

Getting to Know Places

You won't want an adult dog whose freedom is limited because he feels uncomfortable in strange places. And so, make a point to take your young puppy anywhere and everywhere with you. Without a doubt, the single most effective and enjoyable socialization procedure is walking your dog on different routes on a regular basis. There is simply no other activity that will prepare your pup for his life ahead in this way.

It is also time to consider taking your pup to a puppy class. This is perhaps one of the most exciting things you can do with your young pup. You will both learn a lot, and have the time of your life. For many owners, puppy school moments are the most cherished memories of spending time with their dog. Don't miss out on this wonderful opportunity. Anyway, you wouldn't want to neglect your puppy's education, would you?

Cats and dogs can become the best of friends. But it helps to introduce them when the dog is a youngster.

Don't Keep Your Puppy a Secret!

Remember, your puppy needs to meet 50 people in your home before he is three months old. Make a point to invite your neighbors and their children over to meet your puppy. Neighborhood children will be less likely to taunt a dog that they know. And of course, when your dog is old enough to go outside, walk your dog on a different route at least once a day so he meets lots of unfamiliar people.

In puppy class, your pup will have ample opportunity to socialize with a variety of different dogs and their owners. Apart from the fun aspect, the off-leash play sessions in puppy classes are essential for your puppy to learn good bite inhibition and develop a soft mouth. Puppy classes also provide a convenient opportunity for you to ask for professional advice on any pressing or potential puppy problems. To find puppy classes in your area, call the Association of Pet Dog Trainers at 1-800-PET DOGS.

Socialization Checklist: Getting to Know Places

Frequent walks	Friends' homes
Trips in the car	Parking lots
Veterinarian's office	Parks
Pet store	Beaches
Grooming shop	

Puppy Biting

Puppies in a litter spend a lot of their time nipping at each other, so it is no surprise that your pup may think this sort of normal puppy play is all right with you. But, just as your puppy must learn to inhibit his bites with his canine playmates, so must he learn to inhibit the use of his mouth with humans. In fact, learning to inhibit his formidable weapons is the most important lesson your dog will learn.

Puppy class is the best night out for you and your dog!

Surprisingly and luckily, the more your puppy bites you the better his bite inhibition as an adult. Each time your pup bites is another opportunity to remind him how sensitive human skin is. On the other hand, a puppy who never bites humans can't learn how sensitive human skin is and how careful he must be.

With this is mind, you don't want to tell your puppy to stop biting altogether until you are sure that he has first had ample opportunity to learn to use his mouth very carefully. Imagine that one day your dog does bite someone, maybe because that person accidentally stepped on his paw. Heaven forbid this happens. But, if it does, it is essential your dog cause as little harm as possible. You want a dog who has superb bite inhibition. So, the first thing is to teach your pup is that human flesh is very sensitive, much more so than his littermate's skin. Your puppy should think about how careful he has to be when play mouthing with you.

Start by playing with your puppy in his long-term confinement area, or tethered to a solid object. If you play with your puppy when he is off-leash and he nips you, you have no way to get control of the situation unless you grab for your pup. This will most likely get him more riled up.

When your puppy goes to bite you, respond to a little nip with "ouch!" Wait a few moments, then try playing again. The force of your pup's next nibble should come down a bit. If not, say "ouch!" again and walk out of the confinement area or away from where your pup is tethered.

Simply leaving the room is an effective punishment for puppies who don't back off when you say "ouch." Now your puppy has nothing else to play with. You want him to think how boring it is when you stop playing with him (because he nipped you). This momentary social banishment is very effective. You are essentially telling your puppy that you will not play with him if he isn't careful with your skin.

After a week or so, the next step is to teach your pup to stop mouthing altogether. Most puppies will naturally decrease the frequency of their nips, especially when you have taught them to inhibit their force. By the time your puppy is four and a half to five months old, it is time to teach him that he should not use his teeth on people at all. Using the same principle as when teaching bite inhibition, you will simply meet any teeth on your skin (no matter how soft) with an "ouch!" and end the play session if he doesn't stop mouthing on you.

Don't Fight Fire with Fire

If your dog nips you, don't yell at him and go face to face to correct him. A hostile response might escalate the confrontation, or it may teach your puppy to hold back and wait to bite someone who isn't able to use force or to scare him enough to stop (like a child). Certainly, don't grab for your dog's muzzle to correct him. This will only teach him not to like hands reaching toward his face.

Adult Dog Socialization

If you're bringing a new adult dog into your home, your major concern is to check out how well socialized the dog is and to strengthen any weak spots.

For example, if you find that this dog is a bit uncomfortable with men in hats, then you must make a concerted effort to help your new dog to learn to love men wearing hats. Invite over one or two friends at a time to meet your new dog. Ask them to bring hats, but not wear them. Have your dog on a leash and have everyone take a seat. Have one friend (without his hat on) hand-feed the dog his dinner. When your dog is comfortable, have your friend show the hat and feed the dog. Then ask him to casually put on the hat and feed the dog. Make an effort to invite over as many as possible of your male friends, one or two at a time, to follow this procedure. Pretty soon your dog will be searching out men wearing hats because he has learned they are a pretty generous bunch.

For a brush-up, read and follow the socialization exercises outlined in the puppy section.

Maintaining Socialization

Socialization is on-going for the rest of your dog's life. Your dog may have gone to a puppy class (yippee!), and a lucky dog is walked to the park each day. But, while this dog *has* met a number of people and a number of dogs, it is also likely that he will meet those same familiar faces each and every day. To keep your dog socialized he must continue

Doggy Dates

Set up as many safe, off-leash play sessions as possible so your dog can make friends. This is one of the best ways to maintain your dog's socialization to other dogs.

to meet new dogs and new people. The two best ways to do this are walking a different route each day and having parties in your home.

Problems Caused by Failure to Socialize

Socializing your dog is so easy and so much fun that a lot of people fail to take it seriously. However, without adequate socialization, your dog may become fearful and is likely to develop two of the most serious and hard-to-resolve problems, biting and fighting.

It's sad to see a dog who is afraid of people.

Fear or Aggression with People

Reward-based techniques are the method of choice when dealing with fearful or aggressive dogs. If you have a dog who's a little afraid of or doesn't like people, you need to find a way to get the message to the dog, "hey buddy, I like you. If you just come close, I'll give you a bit of kibble." Obviously, using the food as a lure is an effective way to communicate when the dog is afraid of your voice or physical contact (in which case you cannot praise or pat). But it is easy to toss a piece of kibble to the ground.

Make sure you socialize your dog to people and teach him how to greet visitors.

Eventually the dog will come closer, lured by the kibble first on the ground and then in your hand.

Try the following technique: Sit in an armchair and scatter food around you (or your friend). Your dog can approach and retreat as he likes. As he comes closer, he gets the food and as he runs off he gets nothing. Once he is more interested in the lure, you can now take the food and talk to the dog in the language that he has learned; come here, sit, and down. This in itself is like a behavioral pacifier and will accelerate the bonding process.

If you think your dog is fearful, stressed or worried, for your dog's sake please work on this problem. It's no fun being anxious. If you think your dog has any kind of aggression problem, seek help immediately from a professional trainer (call 1-800-PET-DOGS).

Over-Protective Owner

Avoid being overly protective of your puppy or dog, especially if you have a little dog. More often than not, over-protectiveness serves to create or exacerbate fear and aggression problems.

Canine Squabbles

If your dog is unfriendly with lots of other dogs, it means he is not adequately socialized to dogs. (But don't expect your dog to be best friends with every dog, after all we aren't with every person!) A well-socialized dog may still chase, hump and argue. However, socialization ensures your dog has the requisite social savvy to enjoyably and confidently interact with unfamiliar dogs that he may meet and to resolve arguments with other dogs without doing damage. It is easiest to socialize your dog when he is young, but it is never too late to make him more dog friendly.

Don't Make Matters Worse

Dog to dog aggression is most often inadvertently trained in by owners. When an owner sees another dog and tightens the leash, the owner's tension is often relayed to their dog. The dog growls, the owner tightens the leash more and maybe yells at the dog. Over time, the dog becomes conditioned to get tense, as he makes the association between other dogs approaching and his owner's anxiety. So now the dog wants the other dog to stay away, and one of the ways he tries to accomplish this is by growling and barking.

Furthermore, if your dog is uncomfortable with another dog, tightening the leash excludes flight from his possible options and leaves him with fight as the major option. Tightening the leash also distorts your dog's body language and all but forces him to lean forward on his front feet—a posture that the other dog may perceive as somewhat threatening.

Obviously, keep your dog on leash for safety, but you've got to learn to control your dog without tightening the leash. By keeping the leash loose and acting calm, you may convince your dog to do the same! Think about using a head halter—this is one time when it could be very handy.

Don't punish your dog for barking or growling at other dogs. The punishment may teach your dog "I don't like being around other dogs because I am punished whenever they show up, so I'll bark to keep them away.'"

Instead, try to focus on making your dog enjoy the presence of other dogs by associating them with things he likes.

Lack of proper socialization means your dog will never get to fully enjoy fun and games with other dogs.

For dog-to-dog fear or aggression, the method of choice is reward training, and the best feedback is kibble and praise. Start by hand-feeding your dog and getting him fixated on an object (like a Kong or white sterilized bone). This way, you can expose him to one dog (or person) at a time, at a safe distance and give him something to do, such as chewing a toy or eating his kibble. It will give him something to focus on and associate the presence of dogs with things he likes.

The technique here is to go outside and sit on a park bench. Whenever you see another dog you say "oh, look, here comes a cookie

When your dog is under-socialized, everyday encounters can be extremely stressful.

dog." And as soon as your dog sees the other, you give him a treat.
Even if your dog is tense and growling and one might say that you are
rewarding the dog for growling and acting badly around other dogs,
things will improve quickly. The dog cannot help but make the positive association between the approaching dog and the cookie and soon
it will look forward to other dogs approaching. Any time your dog acts
appropriately when a dog approaches, offer a reward. Be sure you give

Nothing makes a dog more reactive than a tight leash. And screaming at him only makes him worse.

your dog enough space from the other dog to feel safe and comfortable. And watch for early signs of discomfort, such as yawning, and excessive panting or activity. You don't want to push your dog too far too fast.

A variation of this would be to get very happy whenever another dog passes by. Your dog cannot fail to make the association between the appearance of another dog and your positive change of mood.

This is important because it is the owner's change in mood that has caused most of the problem. If the dogs where left to their own devices, they would probably resolve the problem amicably.

Every Big Journey Starts with a Tiny Step

If your dog is afraid of people or other dogs, it may take a bit of time for him to regain his confidence. These situations require as much compassion and patience as when dealing with human fears and phobias.

By rewarding your dog in the presence of other dogs, your dog will soon associate the presence of other dogs with rewards.

Basic Manners

The four cornerstones of the foundation of your pet dog's basic manners are sit, down, stand (the position changes) and the notion of closeness. By teaching these four things, you will be able to show him how to behave in nearly any circumstance. For example, you can ask him to sit to greet people politely, to lay down quietly when the family is eating, and to happily stand still while being examined by a veterinarian or groomer. Similarly, teaching your dog the desire to be close is the very essence of teaching your dog to walk calmly by your side down a busy street, and to come back to you when you call him.

When teaching basic manners, keep in mind the principles of dog-friendly dog training.

1. Always concentrate on teaching your dog what you want him to do. Remember, a reliable sit, down or stand will prevent just about any behavior problem.

The building blocks of basic manners are sit, down, stand and the desire to be close.

2. Until your dog is reliably trained, manage his lack of education by, for example, keeping him on leash and out of trouble.

3. Use gentle methods to teach your dog quickly and enjoyably.

WHY TRAIN YOUR DOG?

A well-trained dog will get much more out of life. You'll be able to take your dog just about anywhere with you and bask in the pride you'll feel when your well-trained dog is admired by one and all.

Shirking the responsibility of training your new dog will only mean you will have to make a greater effort later on. Teaching your dog to respond to a few simple requests, such as sit, down and come is a great way to show him what you expect. This way you can tell him what to do to be "right" in any given situation. For example, you can ask him to sit to greet people, rather than jump on them; you can ask him to lay down on his bed while your family eats dinner, rather than get upset with him for begging at the table; you can ask him to come to you when you call, rather than get angry with him for running after the cat.

When you think about it, it would be really cruel *not* to train your dog. Training consists of showing your dog what you want

Did you get a dog so that your backyard could have a pet?

him to do. It's too bad that many dogs are severely punished for behaviors their owners consider inappropriate, only because the

The trained dog gets to be an integral part of the family.

owners didn't bother to show the dogs what was expected. The poor dogs end up being punished for breaking rules they didn't even know existed. All because of a lack of a little education and guidance.

English veterinarian and animal behaviorist, Dr. Ian Dunbar, considers training to be no different from teaching your dog ESL, English as a Second Language. You're not teaching your dog to come, sit and lie down. Four week-old-old puppies know how to come, sit and lie down. Instead, you're teaching your dog the human words for dog behaviors and actions. Wouldn't it be unfair to invite a social animal into your home only to relegate it to a communication-void in solitary confinement? Of course you must socialize and communicate with your doggy companions. And rather than attempting to communicate using a

Training Happens All the Time

Training is not just time "set aside" for your dog's lessons. It's part of everyday life. In fact, your dog is learning every waking moment, whether you are there or not.

variety of dog languages, employing odors, body postures and tail wags, training conveniently enables you to talk to your dog in your language.

PREPARING TO TEACH

Good teachers prepare for class by creating a lesson plan and preparing the classroom. This is the best way to optimize their students' learning potential. A little preparation on your part will facilitate your dog's achievement of his full potential.

Carefully Choose the Classroom

You should carefully choose the environment where you begin teaching your dog. Eventually, you'll want your dog to respond to your requests under all sorts of conditions, but when you begin teaching something new, it's best to train in an area with as few distractions as possible. This is usually in the quietest room in your home.

Precisely Define the Words You Teach Your Dog

You should have a clear picture in your mind of what you are setting out to teach. Your lesson plan will be a precise definition of each word you intend to teach your dog. You don't have to use the same definitions I'm using here (I have included some alternatives), but it is important that you know precisely what you're trying to teach *before* you try to teach.

For example, your dog's name might mean to "pay attention," which may be assessed by whether or not he quickly and reliably follows your instructions. Alternatively, his name might mean that he is supposed look at you, which may be precisely and objectively measured by the speediness and duration of response. "Sit" might mean for your dog to immediately place his bottom on the ground exactly where he is and remain there until the next instruction is given, regardless of the situation and the level of distractions. "Down" might mean for your dog to immediately place his body on the ground exactly where he is and remain there until the next instruction is given, regardless of the situation and the level of distractions. "Walking nicely by your side" might mean there should be no tension on the leash and the dog remains on one side of you. "Come" when called might mean to immediately run to you and to either sit or remain close enough for you to grab his collar.

Also think about how to apply the basic commands in everyday life so that you and your dog get the full benefit of this shared language.

REASONS TO TEACH SIT, DOWN AND STAND
Sit

Most people can think of at least a few reasons for teaching their dog to sit. For example, you want your dog to sit instead of jumping on people or to sit rather than running out the door. There are, however, many uses for this position. In fact, teaching a reliable sit is probably the most underrated and underused command in the doggy world. Aside from socialization, sit is the best way to prevent and solve just about any behavior problem, including housetraining, lunging on leash, chewing inappropriate items, harassing the cat and barking. "Sit" is really good news.

Good Times to Sit

At the front door (going in and out)

When greeting people

While meals are being prepared

In elevators

Every 20 to 30 feet on a walk

Before being let off leash

Frequently during play sessions and games

Before you throw a tennis ball or Frisbee

Before all good times (such as couch privileges)

Down

Generally, down is used to instruct your dog to remain in position for longer periods of time, such as in the living room while guests are getting settled and a lot of activity is happening. Down is also an aid for housetraining. By asking your dog to settle down for a lengthy period of time, you can accurately predict when he needs to go to his doggy toilet (when he gets up) and take him there to reward him when he goes. Down may also be used as an emergency command (for example, if your dog gets off leash, you can ask him to down to get him under control and back on leash), and to prevent a whole slew of unwanted and annoying behaviors.

Good Times to Down

Whenever a sit would be inappropriate (such as when you need the dog to be stationary for a long period of time)

Every 20 to 30 feet on walks

To calm down an overexcited dog

In the waiting room at the veterinarian's office

During your mealtimes

Stand

Stand, of course, is the easiest position for examining and grooming your dog. If your dog stands still, your veterinarian and groomer will absolutely love you.

It's vital to teach a third position change. Stand is a wonderful choice. If you just teach sit and down and you are alternating between them (sit, down, sit, down, as in doing puppy push-ups), the dog learns to anticipate the next position. If he is sitting, the next position will be down. In this case, your dog doesn't actually learn the meaning of the words, just that one behavior leads to the next predictable behavior. But if you are teaching three positions at a time, your dog has to wait for the appropriate instruction. With three possible body positions to choose from, from each position there are a possible two you might ask for. For example, from a sit, you can ask your dog for a down or stand; from a down you can ask for a sit or stand, and from a stand you can ask for a sit or down. So, by teaching three position changes at a time, you are actually training the dog to pay attention and really learn what the words mean.

Good Times to Stand

When being examined at the veterinarian's office

When being bathed and groomed

What's in a Name?

One of the most important words to define for your dog is his name. When you say your dog's name, it should mean that you want him to pay attention and look at you since you are about to give him verbal instructions or a hand signal. Too many dogs think their name means bad dog. Be sure not to use your dog's name only when you're unhappy with him. Moreover, if you repeat your dog's name over and over without any consequence, he will eventually learn to tune you out. Be sure to praise and reward your dog when he responds to his name by looking at you to see what is coming next. Your dog will quickly learn to look at you to find out what opportunities you may be offering.

Six Position Changes

Remember that when teaching three body positions, you're actually teaching six position changes. Some are easier or more difficult than others. For example, it's easy to get a dog to stand and lie down when sitting; it is much harder to get him to sit when lying down and to lie down from the standing position. Luckily, Lure/Reward training makes the process as easy as possible, and there is no better way to teach rapid position changes.

Attention Everyone!

Before you can teach your dog anything, you must first be sure you can get your dog's attention. If you've followed the advice in Chapter One on controlling the resources in your dog's life, you'll find that your dog is already paying a whole lot of attention to you. Also, encourage your dog to make eye contact with you several times

It helps to be animated if you want to capture your dog's attention.

throughout the day, praising for even momentary glances initially. Eventually, you should be able to get your dog's attention even in distracting circumstances. But start to teach this in your home, without a lot of distractions.

The best way to teach your dog to pay attention when you say his name is to hand-feed him his dinner kibble for a week. This doesn't mean that you have to hand-feed each and every piece of kibble, but the more pieces you individually hand-feed, the more dramatic the difference you will see in your dog's responsiveness.

Sit in a chair with your dog's bowl in your hand. Say his name, praise him when he looks at you and give him a piece of kibble. If you need to use a treat or other lure to get your dog to look up and into your face, that's fine. Just move the kibble to your face and praise your dog for looking at you. After a few repetitions, move the food to your face and then move it away from your face. At this point, only reward your dog for looking at you not at the food.

Once your dog readily responds to his name by glancing at you, now it is time to up the ante and to delay giving him the food for progressively longer and longer times. For example, although initially a quick glance in your direction in response to his name was sufficient attention for a reward, now require your dog to look at you for

2 seconds before rewarding him. Next time, wait for him to look at you for 3 seconds. And then 5 seconds, 8 seconds, 10 seconds and so on. Before you know it, your dog won't take his eyes off you.

When he starts to get the idea, repeat the above without food or other rewards on your person. Instead, say his name and when he looks at you, praise and then occasionally *go get* a reward.

Remedial Action

What if your dog doesn't look at you when you say his name? Ignore him and play with a toy he likes a lot. If he tries to join in, continue to ignore him. Or produce something yummy and eat it yourself. Then try again!

Now move to different rooms in the house. When you move into areas with more distractions, you'll need to increase the rewards until he gives you attention there. Your goal is to teach your dog to look at you when he sees a distraction, as it is an opportunity for more reinforcement.

Training Game for Attention

Have a friend or family member as your assistant in this game. Give her some food to hold. You have something your dog loves in your pocket. Sit in two chairs a few feet apart. Have your assistant show your dog the food distraction, but she must not give it to the dog. When the dog is distracted by the food, say your dog's name. If your dog looks at you, give lots and lots of praise and offer the high-level reward you were hiding, *plus* take the food distraction from your assistant and give it to your dog as an additional reward (you can use very small pieces).

If your dog does not look at you, walk over to him and show him what you had to offer him. Let him know how bad you feel for him that he missed out on getting it. Sit down and completely ignore your dog for a few minutes. Then have your assistant distract him again, and you say his name again. Chances are that this time you will get his full attention. By having your assistant never actually giving your dog any food, she is helping you to show him that it is no good to pay attention to distraction. You are the only slot machine that is producing in this casino!

The Release Word

Unless you expect your dog to look at you or stay in a position forever, you'll need to choose a word that means he is released and is essentially on his own time. A lot of people use the words "okay" or "all done." From here on in, you will be teaching your dog that the only times he may release himself is when you have given another command, or his release word. The clearer you are in this regard, the easier you will make things for your dog. It will confuse him if you allow him to sometimes get up from a sit before you have said the release word and then other times you get frustrated and reprimand him for doing so.

Yo-Yo recalls are a wonderful way to attract your dog's attention.

A great way to teach your dog that training is fun is by ignoring your dog when you release him. You want your dog to beg for you to ask him to do something else so he has another opportunity to be rewarded. You want a dog who loves to be in the training game, not a dog who anticipates being released.

Preparation Checklist: Teaching the Basics

1. Carefully choose the classroom.

2. Precisely define the words you teach your dog.

3. Teach your dog to pay attention when you say his name.

4. Teach your dog a release word.

If you've accomplished all four of the above, then you and your dog are ready to move on.

There are a number of gentle, dog-friendly methods for teaching your dog the basics:

1. Lure/Reward Training

2. Reward Training

3. Gentle Physical Prompting

THE THREE METHODS FOR TEACHING SIT, DOWN AND STAND

Lure/Reward Training

Sit

Basically, by luring your dog to move his nose, the rest of his body will follow. So, if you slowly lift a food lure upward and backward over your dog's nose to pass between his eyes, as your dog looks up to follow the food, his rear end will descend into the sitting position. Say "sit" before you move the lure, and give the food each time he sits. Say your release word quickly, before he gets up. Practice this with him at your side and in front of you.

Down

To get your dog to lie down, say "down," hold your hand in front of his nose and move the lure straight down to the ground. Your dog's nose will follow the lure, and so will his forequarters. Usually a dog will completely lie down at this point. If he does, say "good dog" and give him the piece of kibble. If, however, the dog's nose and forequarters go down but his rear end is still sticking up in the air, just push the food lure towards his chest a little and as your dog pushes back to sniff, his rear end will collapse to the ground.

It may take a few tries to get your dog to lay down. Try working on a slippery surface to begin. This will make it much easier to get your dog to slide to the ground. But, do not let him have the lure until he is lying down. He can sniff at your hand, but keep it closed around the food lure. Don't say anything. He will eventually lie down, and then you can open your hand to give him the food. Release him and repeat the routine many times over.

There is a trick for luring little or short-legged dogs into a down. Simply place your dog at the top of a flight of stairs, position yourself one step down. Use your hand with the lure to guide the dog's head below the stair. After a few repetitions on the stairs, you and your pooch are ready to try it on a flat surface.

You can also entice your dog to lie down by luring him to crawl under your bent leg. This works especially well with short-legged dogs.

Stand

To teach your dog to stand on command, say "stand" and move the food from in front of the dog's nose to where his nose would be if he were standing. If your dog does not stand up, waggle the kibble a little, and he soon will.

THE SIX POSITION CHANGES

Stand to Sit

Sit to Down

Down to Stand

Stand to Down

Down to Sit

Sit to Stand

Rover Rollover

Teaching your dog to roll over is a gentle way to get him to be comfortable with and even enjoy being in a vulnerable position. The Lure/Reward method is the best choice for teaching a dog to rollover. Lure your dog into a down, and then use the lure to guide his head to the ground so he's lying flat on one side. Now move the lure over your dog's shoulder so he must twist his neck a bit to follow it. When his feet start to go up, move the lure a little more quickly. When he rolls all the way over, open your hand and give him a small piece of the lure as a reward while he's still laying down. Once your dog has begun to quickly roll over when you use your hand to lure him, add the words "roll over" as you lure your dog. Remember that this is a vulnerable position for your dog to be in, so don't lose patience if it takes a little while for him to feel confident enough to rollover.

Reward Training

One neat thing about this method is that at the beginning, you don't need to give a single verbal instruction. You're letting your dog know "I've got something you want here, what do you think you have to do to get it?" And then, you just wait until the dog works it out himself and gets it right. It's a fun little game, and dogs love it.

Another neat thing about Reward Training is that every time your dog sits and you say the release word and take a step to get him to break the sit (so you can practice it again), your dog walks by your side looking up at you. If you now start taking more than 1 step (2, 3, 5 or 10) between the sits, you will find that in just a few minutes you have taught your dog to walk by your side looking up at you on a loose leash and to sit automatically when you stop.

Basically, Reward Training is the method of choice for rambunctious dogs, fearful dogs and aggressive dogs (in other words, dogs who don't like being touched). The technique is so simple. Although time-consuming at first, once you get going, training will move along like gangbusters. This is a great way to train. To begin, you have eliminated the verbal instructions from the sequence and instead trained your dog to respond to body cues. And because you are using the dog's language—body language—this is a very easy way for your dog to learn.

The wonderful thing about Reward training is that you just amuse yourself and wait for your dog to figure out what you want.

Sit

Hold a little bag with your dog's kibble in it and just wait for him to sit. Don't say a word to your dog, let him figure out what he has to do to get what you have. You can speed things up if you keep your dog on a leash. (Step on it so it's just long enough for your dog to comfortably stand, sit and lie down.) If you just stand still, your dog is likely to throw his entire behavioral repertoire at you—he'll paw, bark, and so on. Ignore behaviors other than sitting. The first sit may take three minutes or more, but don't lose your patience during this initially slow part of an otherwise rapid process. Pretty soon he'll sit. Praise him and give him a piece of kibble when he does.

Now, say the release word and take one step to "reactivate" your dog and wait for him to sit again. The sit should occur in a little less time than the last. By the time you have done 6 to 10 sits, this dog will be sitting instantaneously each time you stop. He will have figured out the "button to push" to get you to release a piece of kibble.

Now that you can predict when your dog will sit (when you stop), you are ready to say "sit" beforehand and praise your dog when he does!

How Many Miles Per Gallon, How Many Sits Per Kibble?

Get the most out of your dog's food. Most owners go to the kitchen and prepare their dog's dinner while he goes crazy bouncing all over. Then, the owner rewards this behavior by giving the dog dinner. Instead, ask your dog for a few sit, stand, and down repetitions before you give him his dinner. Better yet, spend five minutes using a few individual pieces of kibble to get your dog to play the training game with you. See how many sits or downs you can get for each piece.

Down and Stand

The technique for the sit applies also to down and stand. Simply wait for your dog to "give" you these behaviors, and promptly reward him for doing so.

Physical Prompting

Many people are familiar with the techniques to physically prompt a dog to sit, down and stand. If done correctly, the dog learns when gently touched on the rump or when gently touched between his shoulders to assume the appropriate position. At first, the methods seem to get a quick response, but, in fact, Physical Prompting is surprisingly time-consuming, as training becomes a two-step process. Yes, your dog may quickly learn the position changes when close enough for you to touch him. But, you still have to teach your dog to respond to verbal commands and/or hand signals when he is off-leash or at a distance—when you can't get your hands on him to prompt. This becomes a very lengthy task once your dog is responding to touch cues. Because touch is so important to dogs, your

When done correctly, Physical Prompting involves a gentle touch.

Practice, Practice, Practice

Once you've taught your dog position changes, you can practice many, many times throughout the day. Short training sessions (5 to 10 seconds long) are best. Just ask your dog to come and do a few position changes for one piece of kibble, or for the privilege of getting on the couch, or before you throw a tennis ball.

One of the drawbacks of Physical Prompting is that dogs learn they can do what they like when they are out of reach.

Sit!
Sit!
Sit!
Sit!

Maintain a Good Attitude

Your dog's enthusiasm for learning depends greatly on you, so never try to train if you're irritable.

dog will selectively attend to the touch. In effect, he doesn't even hear the instructions you give. It is much more effective to teach your dog verbal commands from the outset using Lure/Reward training.

Hands-off Reward methods create a good foundation for off-leash distance control.

Physical prompting is seldom recommended to begin teaching position changes. However, the best thing about this method is that it does incorporate a lot of gentle handling if you are doing it pro-perly. It is important that your dog enjoys having you touch him all over. So, once you have Lure/Reward or Reward trained your dog, it's a great idea to practice gently molding him into positions using physical prompting.

Sit

To get your dog to sit, say the word "sit," and then gently apply pressure to your dog's rear end, or use your hand to tuck in his rear by applying pressure just above his hocks.

Down

You can position your dog into a down by having him sit and then gently taking his elbows to lift his front feet and then lowering him down, or gently applying pressure between his shoulder blades as you lure him down with a piece of food.

Stand

Ask your dog to stand, and use your hand in his collar or on a leash to gently guide him into this position while you put your other hand in front of one of his hind legs to keep him from walking forward.

Stay

The use of a word to tell your dog to stay is actually repetitive if you have already decided to teach your dog that the words "sit," "down," and "stand" mean to stay in position until released or asked to do something else. But feel free to use the word "stay" if it makes you happy.

Sit-stay is useful when something is going on and you need short-term control. Stand-stay is good for having your dog stand still for an examination or grooming. Down-stay is useful for long-term control.

Using the Lure/Reward method, all you need to do is hold the lure steady and delay giving it to your dog stand for progressively longer and longer periods of time. For example, ask your dog to sit, and reward him when he does it. The next time, wait for your dog to remain sitting for a full second before offering the food reward. If your dog gets up beforehand, just repeat the process until he gets it right. The next time, wait for 2 seconds of sitting before offering a reward. Then, go for 3 seconds, 5, 8, 10, 15, 20, and so on. It will surprise you how quickly your dog learns quite lengthy stays.

Using the Reward Method, just wait to reward for the sits, downs or stands that are longer. Pure simplicity!

Using Physical Prompting, place your dog in position. If he tries to move gently put him back in the required position.

Proofing Stays

Proofing your dog's stays comprises:

1. Increasing the duration

2. Increasing the distractions

3. Increasing the distance (between you and your dog)

You need to work on each component separately. Eventually, your dog will understand that he is to stay in a position for an extended period of time around heavy distractions while a distance away from

Doubles Anyone?

Playing the training game with two handlers at once can be very helpful, especially if you are working on distance and distractions. One person can stay next to the dog to help and reward him, while the other person moves a distance away and/or causes distractions.

you. Building duration, distance and distraction is like turning up the volume on a stereo. If you raise the level too high too fast, your dog won't be able to concentrate on what you are asking him to do. Make things easier on you and your dog: Go slowly.

Increasing the Duration

By simply delaying giving the reward, you will increase the length of time your dog stays in the required position. Hold on to that piece of kibble for 5 seconds and praise your dog. Then, see if you can hold on to the kibble for 7 seconds. If your dog gets up, either ask him to go back into the position (sit, down or stand) again, or simply ignore him and wait for him to figure it out. (This is another time when it's good to have your dog on a leash that you're stepping on or that's connected to a stationary object.)

Get a stopwatch and see who in the family can get your dog to remain in each position for the longest amount of time. You can put on your own weekly Stay Olympics!

Increasing Distractions

Start training your dog with as few distractions as possible. Then, gradually increase them, one by one, until your dog responds willingly no matter what the distraction.

Stay right next to your dog when you begin teaching positions, and periodically reward him (a tiny piece of a kibble or treat will do). When he can stay for 30 seconds or so, try adding a very mild distraction. What is considered mild will vary from dog to dog. For some dogs, the presence of a tennis ball rolling across the floor is enough to send them skyrocketing to the moon, while others wouldn't bat an eye. You know your dog best, so start off with something he isn't very interested in.

As you add distractions, increase the rewards and decrease the length of time. For example, for a dog who is just able to do a nice 30-second sit without new distractions, ask for a 3-second sit during the presence of a tennis ball. At the same time, lavishly praise him and offer a nice food reward for his success.

Remember, stays are much harder for your dog in the presence of a single distraction. So, keep the distance and duration short, and up the level of rewards.

Increasing Distance

When you want to work on building up the distance you can walk away from your dog while he is sitting or lying down, remove distractions and decrease the length of time you ask him to hold a position.

When proofing stays, increase your distance from your dog gradually and progressively.

Move just one foot away, and praise your dog if he stays. If he gets up, just step back and ask him to sit or down again or wait for him to do so. Take a tiny step away again, and go right back to praise and reward him if he stays put. The next time, step away 2 steps for a short period. Then try 3 steps, 5, 8, 10, and so on until it is possible to walk well away and your dog stays put.

Gradually increase the distance you move away, and don't forget to increase the rewards as you ask for more reliability. If at any point your dog gets up, don't get mad at him. Calmly ask him for the appropriate position once more.

If you don't have a friend or family member to assist you, tie your dog to a stationary object like a fence. Start just a foot or so away, and ask your dog to do a few sit, stand, down repetitions. By tying your dog, you are freeing up your hands to give clear signals and removing the possibility that you'll get tangled up in a long leash!

JUST TO BE CLOSE TO YOU

Instilling in your dog the desire to be close to you is at the heart of teaching him to come when you call and walk nicely by your side on

Time and Training

Keep training sessions short, and stop while your dog still wants to play the training game. Little and often is the best policy. Twenty-five two-minute training sessions a day will give you and your dog ample opportunity to build up reliability, even around enticing distractions. It isn't very realistic or effective to set aside an hour-long training session for your dog each day. This can make the process seem long and boring for you and your dog. Having a specific training time is great, but remember that your dog is really being trained every waking moment, whether you're there or not.

leash. Because proximity is a sign of affection and confidence, you will have a much easier time teaching your dog to come close (recall) and to stay close (walk nicely on leash) if he trusts, likes and wants to be near you. If your dog completely ignores you or runs away when you call him, it tells you where you are in the relationship. In this case, you simply need to give yourself and your dog a chance at a fresh start. If you have lived together for a while, pretend as though you just brought him home and follow the instructions below. Using dog-friendly training techniques all but assures that you and your dog will have a loving and trusting bond and that your dog will want to be close. A dog who likes to be close to you and has been adequately rewarded for doing so, will respond enthusiastically when you call him to come or to walk by your side.

It's very easy to instill in young puppies a desire to be close that will carry through to adulthood. Puppies under $4^1/_2$ months old have a strong tendency to follow anything that moves away. It is wise to imprint off-leash control before this time. If your pup doesn't come happily to you by $4^1/_2$ months, then you better get on the ball.

Off and On Switch

Stop play sessions often to ask your dog to sit or down before starting play again. You'll ensure that you can get your dog's attention even in the height of excitement. Moreover, excited play becomes a reward rather than a distraction.

Come When Called

Teaching your dog to come when called is one of the most important obedience exercises you'll ever teach. It's the best way to allow your dog to safely enjoy off-leash fun, but more importantly a good recall is the best way to avoid potential disasters. The consequences of a dog who ignores you when off leash can be devastating. Your goal with this exercise is to teach your dog to come to you even in the face of very enticing distractions. You are teaching him that it is always better to go to you than anything or anyone else.

Sit at the End

At the end of the recall, it is a good idea to add on a sit. Why? Because if you have a motivated recall, a medium or large dog will flatten you. So make sure your dog knows to end up in a sit. This means you should say "sit" (and help with a hand signal) when your dog is about three dog lengths away from you so he can slow down in anticipation of sitting.

Choose and Use Your Recall Word Wisely

The word you use to ask your dog to come to you should be considered special, so choose it carefully. If you have a dog with whom you have already used the word "come" and he ignores it, then you may want to choose a new word and start fresh.

Your dog's life may someday depend on his knowing to come to you when called, so don't ruin his recall word by using it before you have taught your dog what it means. Start by only saying this word when you're as sure as possible that your dog will respond. Do not begin by using it when your dog is off leash in an area where you are less interesting than the environment, or another dog's rear end! If he chooses not to respond, then you have allowed your dog at least one opportunity to learn that he doesn't have to respond. Instead, keep your dog on leash or in a safely enclosed area until you have taught him to come when called. Also, don't call your dog if you are about

Guaranteed Recall

Call your dog at least five times a day for a week when you're sure he will come. This usually means in the house at a close distance, or when he is already coming toward you. Reward him with the best things to happen to him that day (play, hugs, treats, a walk).

to do something he finds unpleasant, such as bathe him, clip his nails or take him home from a run in the park. Instead, calmly walk over, get a hold of his collar and give him a treat (which should be easy if you've practiced handling your dog. This way you avoid associating the recall with unpleasant things and thereby increase the chance that your dog will respond to you when you do call him (especially in an emergency) in the future.

Hide and Seek

No matter which techniques you choose to use to teach your dog to come when called, you should make things easier on you and your dog by instilling in your dog the desire to keep his eye on you and want to come close. Playing hide and seek with your dog is a great way to do this.

There are two variations of hide and seek, both are great for the whole family to play. The first variation has the greatest impact on puppies under 4½ months old, because they are so impressionable. It is best to play this game in a safely enclosed area, preferably your yard. The next best option is a friend's yard. Let your puppy get distracted from you and when he does, run and hide. Wait until he notices you are gone and looks con-cerned. Give him a few moments to try and find you. When you see he is really con-cerned, make a little noise to give him an idea of where you are. After a few moments, jump out and let your puppy know where you are. Hug him and praise him when he finds you. This exercise is almost one-trial learning. Your dog will learn that sticking close to you is important, because you have a tendency to get lost!

Hiding from your dog in safe places is one of the best exercises to teach him to pay attention and keep close.

The second variation can be played indoors or outdoors in a safely enclosed area. When your dog is distracted, call his name and then run and hide. If you can't "lose" your dog, put something on the floor (a toy or kibble) to distract him and then run and hide. To begin, hide in a spot where your dog will find you easily. As he gets the knack of the game, you can hide in a spot were he has to look a little harder to find you.

Ready, Set, Go

Have a friend or family member hold onto your dog as you dash off. Call your dog to you when you get about 20 feet away. When your dog is reliable doing it this way, start to add distractions. Try setting out a couple of toys that your dog must pass on his way to get to you. When he does get to you, reward him by having even better toys for him to play with.

Lure/Reward Training

Stand or sit in a chair across from a family member or friend. Call your dog to you and encourage him to come toward you by showing him a lure (toy or kibble). Praise him starting with the very first step he takes in your direction. When he gets to you, give him a piece of kibble. Then have the person in the chair opposite you call him the same way. To keep the game interesting, have a few different rewards to offer and don't repeat this more than six times in a given play session. Move farther and farther apart, and continue to reward. But, as your dog gets better at this game, reward randomly and keep him guessing about when he will be rewarded and what the reward will be.

Another Lure/Reward technique is to find a friend with a well-trained dog. Call your dog and then have your friend, who should be standing next to you, call her dog immediately after. Her dog will come running and your dog will follow! Pretty soon your dog will get the idea, and you can speed both dogs up by rewarding the first one to get to you with a treat. By doing this, you will get some very fast moving dogs. If one dog simply can't move as quickly as the other, you can level the playing field by waiting until the slower dog is closer to you when you call them.

Reward Training

This method could be called No Call Recalls! As with all Reward training, this process is so easy you may not believe it works until you see it for yourself. All you need to do is wait for your dog to approach you and give him a piece of kibble when he does. There is no need to call him to you. He will learn that the simple act of heading in your direction is likely to produce a very happy owner and maybe even a tasty piece of kibble. Be sure to vary how often and what you offer as a reward as this is the best way to keep your dog interested in the training game.

The very best way to speed up recalls; two dogs but only one treat!

After a week or so of practicing this, call your dog once you see that he's heading toward you (this is where the verbal instruction comes in). After another few days, try calling him before he chooses to run to you on his own.

Physical Prompting

A lot of people will teach a dog to come on a long line, and of course using a leash goes far to ensure your dog's safety. It's a great way to practice any outside work with your dog, on a 6-foot leash or on a 30- to 50-foot line. However, I would strongly recommend only to use the leash for safety and not to prompt the dog to come along. As soon as you do this, you are setting yourself up for failure. Everything goes fine when you are doing recalls on leash because when you can sort of drag in the dog like a dead sea bass, you know he is going to

Shake, Rattle and Call

Always have a few bits of kibble in your pocket with your puppy or adult dog in training. If you don't like carrying food around, you can have it in screw-top jars in strategic places like on the fridge, bathroom or in the garden near his doggy toilet. Whenever you pass one of these, you can call the dog and then shake the jar. When he comes, get out a piece of kibble and give it to him. After a while, you'll want to thin out the number of times you shake the jar after you call him and the number of times you give him a piece of kibble. This way, you will have a dog who comes when you call him, even if you don't have a lure on you.

come. This becomes a tremendous crutch in training, and neither you nor the dog are developing off leash skills.

How to Guarantee Your Dog Won't Come

The recall is one of the easiest commands to teach but one of the quickest to trash. Many owners ruin their dog's desire to come when called by doing one or all of the following:

- ◆ Calling the dog when they're angry
- ◆ Calling the dog when they're about to do something he doesn't like (for example, nail clipping and bathing)
- ◆ Calling the dog to put on his leash at the dog park
- ◆ Calling the dog to be put in confinement
- ◆ Waiting to praise the dog until he gets to them
- ◆ Not rewarding the dog sufficiently
- ◆ Calling their off-leash dog to come before he is trained
- ◆ Obviously, don't do any of these!

Call your dog often during off-leash play sessions. When he comes back to you, let him know

When your dog is on a long line, it is possible to safely teach recalls in public places.

When a dog doesn't come when called, first catch the dog. Second, for his own safety, please don't let him off leash again until you have trained him to be more reliable.

Your dog isn't going to come quickly the next time if you yell at him when he gets there. Always reward your dog when he gets to you.

Maintaining a Great Recall

Don't wait to call your dog in an emergency to find out he isn't trained as well as you thought. Keeping your dog's recall reliable is a top priority. Call your dog to you no less than five times a day, every day, and vary the rewards from verbal praise to a tasty treat or a game of fetch. Remember to praise your dog every step of the way; the most important steps to praise are the first, not the last. Neglecting to praise your dog while he is in the act of heading to you is a surefire way to teach him not to run to you.

how pleased you are and then tell him to go back and play again. You are accomplishing two important things here: checking to make sure your dog complies and teaching your dog that coming to you does not mean the end of play, but rather a pleasant time out for reward.

Be aware! The biggest distraction for all sight hounds (in fact, for most dogs), is a rapidly retreating critter. If you don't yet have a reliable recall, walk your dog on leash.

There are numerous leash techniques to train your dog to stop pulling and walk calmly. When most people think of a dog walking close, they immediately think of leash and collar training—jerking the dog this way and

Even a little dog has a lot of pull!

that to get him to stay by your side. While you can train a dog to walk close using the leash in this way, this method is extremely deceptive. Of course, when you're walking on public property or any place that might be dangerous, you want your dog on leash for safety's sake. But, I would strongly advise you not to use a leash as the only

Come and Get It!

Have a friend or family member hold your dog in another room while you prepare his dinner. Call your dog (tell the person to let go when you do so), and reward him for coming to find you by giving him his dinner.

training aid. If you think about it, the very notion of having to jerk the dog around is antithetical to teaching the dog to want to be close to you.

Indeed, when you train a dog this way, everything appears hunky-dory and looks wonderful until you take the dog off leash.

More importantly, what starts off as gentle physical prompting almost always turns into physical force. Eventually, most dogs become desensitized to leash corrections. So, do not rely on the leash to get the dog to come close or keep close.

What If My Dog Won't Walk?

Never pull your dog if he is scared to walk on leash. Just wait and reward him when he gets to you.

Nothing will make your dog balk and want to move away from you more than jerking the leash and dragging him. If your dog lags, be careful not to reinforce this behavior by giving him attention when he stops. Instead, stand still facing away from your dog and put gentle pressure on the leash and wait. Praise your dog if he moves even one inch to come towards you. Alternatively, go to the end of the leash and kneel down facing away from your dog and wait for your dog to come to you, praising him all the way. It doesn't matter how long it takes (it shouldn't be more than a minute or

The Tie That Binds: Umbilical Cord Training

Leaving a young or new dog to explore the house on his own is asking for trouble. Even being in the same room as your new dog may not be sufficient supervision. It takes very little time for your dog to chew a piece of furniture or soil the carpet. Tying your dog to you (around your waist) is an effective way to allow your dog to spend time with you around the home, under safe and constant supervision when he is not resting in his long-term confinement area. As a bonus, within a few days, your dog will have a habit of walking by your side around the house and settling at your side when you stop.

two), he eventually will. Then, walk another few feet away and repeat if he stops.

If your dog is afraid of leash walking, you want to take him out for numerous confidence building training sessions on leash. You don't want to take him with you on an errand when you may be in a hurry and get frustrated with your dog. Once you have taken the time to teach your dog to enjoy leash walking, he can come along with you on all your errands.

TIME TO RANDOMLY REWARD

Your ultimate goal is to get your dog to respond to you properly without having to reward him every time. Of course, in the pet dog world you don't have to phase out the kibble treats, toys or games entirely because a lot of people like giving their dog rewards. I love occasionally rewarding my dogs; it makes both of us happy. But you do want to know that your dog will comply with your requests even without the presence of food or toys in your hands.

When you can reliably get position changes with a lure in your hand (this should take only a few practice sessions), it is time to begin phasing out food or toys and varying the reinforcement.

There are three themes to randomizing rewards:

1. Keep Your Dog Guessing When (ask for more behaviors for fewer rewards).

2. Keep Your Dog Guessing What (throw a tennis ball instead of giving a treat).

3. Keep Your Dog Guessing Where (rewards come from your pocket, the cupboard, or somebody else).

You'll see these three themes at work in the steps that follow.

5 Steps to Decreasing Use of Lures and Rewards

1. Lure in hand, reward at random.

2. No lure in hand, reward from other hand or from pocket.

3. No lure in hand, reward from other hand or pocket randomly.

4. No lure in hand, no reward in pocket, someone else rewards dog or you get the reward from someplace else.

5. No lure in hand, no rewards in pocket, use life rewards, like continuing a walk, or verbal praise and petting most of the time.

Shout and Treat!

Yell for your dog to come to you, and when he does, lavish him with lots of praise, toys or kibble and a few treats. He'll learn that urgency in your voice doesn't mean you're angry, it just means to get there fast and get hugs and treats! In an emergency situation, you will probably yell at your dog, but if you've practiced this way in non-emergency situations, your dog is much less likely to be spooked if you panic!

More for Less

Start to ask more of your dog for less of a reward. Increase the number of position changes that you expect for one bit of kibble. Continue to use the food lure in your hand for all of the position changes, but no longer give it to him every time. Instead, you will vary when you give it to him and from where it comes. Try taking a bit of food from your pocket, from someone else's, or from the cupboard. This is also a good time to start varying the type and amount of reward you offer. Ask a friend to approach your dog and offer three treats.

Initially, have your dog sit for a bit of kibble, then sit and lie down for kibble, then sit, lie down and stand for kibble, etc. Eventually, you want 10 position changes or so for just one bit of kibble.

To phase out food (or other lures), simply keep the food in your pocket and with an open hand signal your dog. You will find the food lure (hand) movement has become a hand signal and that your dog was actually responding to your hand movement with the lure. So the dog learns hand signals very quickly. You can offer kibble from your pocket as a reward. Make the reward much better than what you used as a lure. If he doesn't sit, simply try again.

Nothing Is Free

Anything your dog wants—food, attention, toys, access to furniture (if he's allowed on it)—should all be controlled and used to get the dog to realize that doing what you ask is the way to reach the end of the reward rainbow.

Hand-feed meals for a week or so, asking him to sit, down and stand for each piece of kibble. When he walks up to you for a scratch, ask him to sit first. When your dog does a few position changes, you throw the tennis ball. Ask your dog to sit before he gets to get on the couch. Ask your dog to lie down before he gets to get in the car for a ride. Eventually, doing these position changes just becomes part of the dog's life, and the dog is internally motivated.

Behavior Problems

I n the wild, dogs live in dens and they have their own way of going about things, The Doggy Way. But if you want your dog to live in your home with you, you must teach him the human way of living. Specifically, you have to teach your dog to redirect his normal and natural doggy behaviors. Failing to learn where to relieve himself, what to chew, when to bark, when to jump up and where to dig are the top reasons why the relationship fails and people give up their dogs. Luckily these techniques are so simple to teach that you and your dog are all but guaranteed to have a long and happy life together.

BARKING NINE TO FIVE

What does a bark mean? Well, what does a word mean? The bark is the dog's word, and it can mean many things. Your dog barks when he's alerting you to an intruder, when he's afraid, when he's playful and when he's bored. Barking is caused by the presence of stimuli

Most behaviors problems are unintentionally encouraged during the first few weeks a puppy or dog is in his new home. For example, this puppy is learning that barking is a good way to be the center of attention.

(strange people, dogs, sights or sounds), the owner's absence, or as an attention seeking mechanism. The easiest way to control barking is to socialize your dog so he's comfortable with lots of people, places and things and to instill in him a strong chewtoy habit so he is mentally and physically exercised and occupied. But, just as you wouldn't attempt to completely silence a person, you shouldn't try to completely silence your dog. Your dog just needs to learn some basic bark control—when to bark and for how long.

Regardless of the reason for your dog barking, your goal is to properly socialize your dog, to teach your dog to focus on something other than barking, and to teach your dog to speak and be quiet on command, so you can control when and for how long he barks.

Alarm Barker

Dogs who bark at the presence of intruders can be a valuable asset. It's ironic that barking dogs are such a problem in our society, inasmuch as barking as an alarm must have been one of the main reasons we domesticated dogs in the first place and one of the reasons we live with dogs today. Usually, it isn't the barking that is a problem, just that the dog is a little too enthusiastic. Most people *want* their dogs to let them know when someone has stepped onto the property. It only becomes a problem if the dog does not settle afterwards.

Teach your dog to bark and be quiet on cue and thereby have an on/off switch for your dog. Invite three friends to come over for a speak-and-shush party, and within 30 minutes you'll have a well-trained barker and shusher.

Have your dog's dinner kibble on hand. Ask your dog to speak (request), instruct your visitors to knock on the door when they hear you say this (lure), and reward your dog by saying "thank you" (reward) when he barks. Your dog may look a bit shocked for a moment. After all, he's probably used to being yelled at when he barks.

Now, to get him to be quiet, say "shush,"(request) and waggle a piece of kibble in front of his nose (lure). Once he sniffs the food, he'll be quiet and so give him the kibble as a reward. Repeat this many times, and your dog will become increasingly aware of how much fun it is to speak on request and how rewarding it is to shush on request.

Yard Barker

Barking dogs are one of the most common complaints of urban and suburban neighbors. Obviously, a dog left outside will alert to all the visual and auditory stimuli.

Dogs are usually relegated to the yard because they're not house-trained or chewtoy trained. If that's the case, housetrain and chewtoy train your dog. Rescue your dog from the backyard and bring him into your home! Giving your dog a few well-stuffed chewtoys is the easiest and most effective solution. This way he has something to think about other than barking. A well-stuffed chewtoy will keep your dog busy for an hour or more (this means no time for barking). If you need to, put his food bowl away and only feed him from his chewtoys. You'll keep him *very* busy!

No Yard Dogs Please

It's not a great idea to leave your dog alone in your yard. Not only will his housetraining and chewtoy manners deteriorate, but he's also likely to learn and engage in other activities you won't appreciate, such as digging, barking, or escaping. Moreover, he's vulnerable to a number of dangers including being stolen, poisoned or hurt by an animal that comes into the yard.

Attention Seeking Barker

When you're relaxed and in a good mood, tie your dog to a secure spot in the house and get a good book to read. Stand or sit next to your dog and ignore him. When he barks, move away. When he's quiet, even for a moment, move closer. Your dog will soon realize barking means you leave and quiet means you return. When he's quiet for 10 to 15 seconds, approach and praise and maybe offer a piece of kibble.

If your dog is barking for your attention . . .

. . . simply teach him it will have the opposite effect.

Owner-Absent Barker

What if your dog barks because he's bored and stressed when left at home alone? Unfortunately, our canine friends are often left alone for long periods of time. Being social animals, it's tough for dogs to understand why their family leaves them. However, you can teach your dog to tolerate and even enjoy your absence.

First, teach your dog to spend time alone when you're home. Most people make the mistake of spending all the time they're home with their dog at their side. While this may seem to be a kind and loving act, it only serves to make matters worse. Your dog will become accustomed to constant companionship and be more likely to fall apart when you leave.

Remember, some dogs have been specifically bred to be companions and they may especially miss you when left at home alone. So, teach them right away to tolerate and even enjoy time by themselves.

Instead, teach your dog to enjoy quiet moments by himself while you're home, so he'll feel more confident when you're not there. Frequently and for short periods of time, confine your dog to another room, his crate or on a tie-down and give him a well-stuffed chewtoy to occupy his time.

Whining

It's best not to attempt to soothe your dog when he whines—this will only serve as reward and you'll actually be reinforcing the whining behavior. Instead, ignore your dog until he's quiet. After a 10 to 15 seconds of silence, calmly let him know you like quiet by offering him a food reward.

Citronella Collars

A wonderful training aid is the Aboistop collar. When your dog barks, the collar squirts a citronella spray in front of your dog's nose. As the dog sniffs, he stops barking. The collar is extremely effective with most dogs.

POSSESSIVENESS

In the dog's mind, resources, like food and bones, are meant to be gathered and protected. But for a pet dog, having this attitude can get him in to a whole lot of trouble. You can help your dog to avoid any potential problems by showing him how rewarding it is to relinquish resources at your request.

Teach Your Dog to Share

Teaching your dog to share can begin in one session of hand-feeding him his dinner kibble. Simply hold

Mine! All mine! (this could be a problem) . . .

a piece of kibble in your closed hand. Ignore your dog when he push-es at your hand to get the food. Wait until he stops and backs off. To begin, even just a momentary "retreat"should be rewarded. Tell him to "take it," and open your hand to give him the kibble. After a few repetitions, add the request "leave it." Say "leave it." present your closed hand, and wait for your dog to back off, then open your hand and say "take it." He'll learn the only way to get the food after you say leave it is to not touch your hand.

Thank You!

You can also teach this by letting your dog sniff and gently chew a toy or bone that you hold in your left hand. Don't choose his favorite toy, start with something that is of a little lower value to him. In your right hand, which is held behind your back, hold a valuable treat. Say "thank you"(or whatever word or phrase you choose) as you bring out your right hand to give your dog the treat from that hand. After several repetitions, your dog will look away from the treat and toward the right hand when you say "thank you."

Teach your dog to enjoy exchanging valued possessions.

After 5 to 10 practice sessions, each consisting of three requests to give, start to teach your dog to respond to the word alone, without the signal of your right hand. Just say the word and wait until your dog looks for your hand and then give him a reward.

Ultimately, you want to diminish the number of times you give your dog the treat. Keep him guessing as to when he'll get it. Continue verbally praising him and offer a food treat or some other reward about 1 out of every 10 requests.

HAS JUMPING UP GOT YOU DOWN?

Dogs jump on people to say "hello" in an effort to be friendly. Although you want your dog to be friendly with people, his over-enthusiasm may keep friends away and make all that wonderful socialization go to waste. Your dog deserves to be taught about how to properly greet people so he can enjoy the pleasure of human company.

Don't try this at home! Your dog can be trained to "give" on request.

Frequently, dogs are reinforced for jumping up during puppyhood. Most jumping up occurs when owners come home and are not in training mode.

Teach your dog to stand or sit to greet people. Invite a few friends over and get your dog's dinner kibble ready. For each person that comes to the door,

Understandably, most people would prefer to be greeted by a dog who has been taught to sit to say "hello."

simply wait for your dog to sit and then give him one piece of his kibble. If each person would be kind enough to leave and come back 10 times, you'll have 30 practice sessions by inviting over just three people. If you want to speed things up a bit, lure your dog into a sit.

People have devised all sorts of ways to physically punish dogs for jumping up, such as jerking the leash, holding the dog's paws, stepping on his hind feet, kneeing him in the chest and flipping him over backward. Why not train the dog how to greet people appropriately? Why not just train him to sit?

When an overly enthusiastic greeting is met with a physical punishment and/or a verbal correction, the dog may be left thinking "I just wanted to say 'hi.' Wow, they must be angry at me. Let me try and make up by greeting them happily again." Indeed, punishments often prompt your dog to jump up with renewed vigor, for which he is then met with a more severe punishment. The act of greeting people now becomes a confusing prospect for your dog. Some dogs with softer temperaments may be so confused and panicked that they actually begin to urinate when greeting people. What is perceived as a disgusting behavior by the owners is actually a way for the dog to say how submissive he feels in the face of potential punishing people.

SEPARATION ANXIETY

Dogs are social creatures who don't like to be left alone. Sadly, most pet dogs spend a large part of their time by themselves. To prepare your dog to enjoy time spent at home alone, make sure he frequently spends time by himself when you're home. You don't want to set a precedent of constant companionship—this just sets your dog up to fall apart when you're gone.

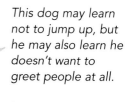

This dog may learn not to jump up, but he may also learn he doesn't want to greet people at all.

Some dogs react to being left alone by indulging in their favorite pastimes. These might include being destructive to the home or themselves, barking, or marking the house with urine and feces.

Many owners have difficulty ignoring their dog during the course of the day, especially when their dog seeks attention. It becomes a habit for them to almost constantly interact with their dog. Try using a crate or a tie-down. A tie-down is a leash that can't be chewed through with a snap either on both ends or just one end. The tie-down should be only about 3 feet long, just enough for the dog to sit, lay down, stand up and turn around. It is sort of like a crate without walls. Put a stuffed Kong or bone in your dog's crate or by the tie-down to give him something to do while he spends some time alone.

GARBAGE RAIDING

To discourage garbage raiding, get a garbage can that has a locking lid. Or, simply put the garbage can in a place your dog can't reach, like under the sink. If you attempt to correct your dog when you catch him raiding the can, chances are that all he will learn is to avoid going on a "garbage hunt" when you're around. You'll essentially have created an owner absent garbage hound.

DIGGING

Terriers dig? Of course they do! Terrier comes from the word terra, meaning earth. Terriers were created, bred and born to dig for hundreds of years.

Your dog has lots of reasons to want to dig. Digging is fun and it relieves boredom. To prevent unwanted digging, don't let your dog spend unsupervised time in the yard. Go outside and watch him play or better yet, play with him.

If you don't want to ban digging, you can teach him that it isn't digging you hate, just digging everywhere. So, choose one spot and designate it as his digging pit. Think of it as his sandbox. Let him watch you bury a couple of tasty chewtoys. Then encourage him to dig in that spot to get them out. Your dog will learn that this is the best (and only) place to dig, because it's where the buried treasure is and because you are there to help him choose the right spot.

HYPERACTIVITY

It's all too common for dog trainers to hear owners describing their dogs as hyperactive. In fact, most of these dogs aren't really hyperactive, they just have the typical energy level of a dog (high) and are in a home where the owner has the typical energy level of a person (not quite as high as the dog, especially after a long day at work).

The simple solution to this "problem" is to make sure your dog has adequate exercise (talk to your vet about the needs of your particular dog), is fed the appropriate food (food affects a dog's behavior, just like it does with people), is mentally stimulated (lots of fun, educational toys like stuffed Kongs hidden around the house), and is taught to have an on/off switch. That is, many times throughout the day, play with your dog and get him into an energetic mood. Interrupt the play many times by asking your dog to lay down (at first luring and then asking with just a hand signal or verbal request). To begin, ask him to lay down for just a few seconds before you release him, and then wait a few moments to play with him again. Gradually increase the length of time you expect him to control himself and stay laying down.

Continually getting him excited and then settling him down turns what could be a problem (an excited, high-energy dog) into a reward for calm behavior. This is a perfect example of a life reward, using something your dog likes which is not concrete (not a treat or praise) to reward him for behavior that you like.

Resource Guide

ASSOCIATION OF PET DOG TRAINERS

This group is the BEST source for finding a trainer in your area and for finding information about dog training seminars. The number is 1-800-Pet-Dogs. Or write to:

Association of Pet Dog Trainers
P.O. Box 3734
Salina, CA 93912

BOOKS

Arden, Andrea. *Train Your Dog the Lazy Way.* New York: Alpha Books, 1998.

Donaldson, Jean. *The Culture Clash.* Oakland, CA: James & Kenneth Publishers, 1996.

Dunbar, Ian, PhD, MRCVS. *Doctor Dunbar's Good Little Dog Book.* Oakland, CA: James & Kenneth Publishers, 1992.

Dunbar, Ian, PhD, MRCVS. *Dog Behavior: An Owner's Guide to a Happy Healthy Pet.* New York: Howell Book House, 1998.

Need more help to build your perfect dog?

Dunbar, Ian, PhD, MRCVS. *How to Teach a New Dog Old Tricks.* Oakland, CA: James & Kenneth Publishers, 1991.

Pryor, Karen. *Don't Shoot the Dog: The New Art of Teaching and Training.* New York: Bantam Books, 1984.

Ryan, Terry. *The Toolbox for Remodeling Your Problem Dog.* New York: Howell Book House, 1998.

VIDEOS

Broitman, Virginia and Sherri Lippman. *Take a Bow...Wow! Easy Tricks Any Dog Can Do.* Doswell, VA: Take A Bow Wow, 1995.

Dunbar, Ian, PhD, MRCVS. *Dog Training for Children.* Oakland, CA: James & Kenneth Publishers, 1996.

Dunbar, Ian, PhD, MRCVS. *Sirius Puppy Training.* Oakland, CA: James & Kenneth Publishers, 1987.

Dunbar, Ian, PhD, MRCVS. *Training the Companion Dog.* (Set of four videos, "Socialization," "Behavior Problems," "Leash Walking and Jumping Up," and "Recalls and Stays.") Oakland, CA: James & Kenneth Publishers, 1992.

Dunbar, Ian, PhD, MRCVS. *Training Dogs with Dunbar: Fun Training for You and Your Dog.* Oakland, CA: James & Kenneth Publishers, 1996.

Hunthausen, Wayne. *Dogs, Cats & Kids.* Donald Manelli & Associates, Inc. 1996.

CATALOGS

Cherry Brook
(General pet supplies)
Route 57, P.O. Box 15
Broadway, NJ 08808
800-524-0820
908-689-7979

Doctors Foster & Smith
(General pet supplies)
2253 Air Park Road
P.O. Box 100
Rhinelander, WI 54501-0100
800-826-7206

Dogwise, Direct Book Service's Dog & Cat Book Catalogue
(Pet books, including rare and hard to find)
P.O. Box 2778
Wenatchee, WA 98807-2778
800-776-2665
509-663-9115
www.dogwise.com

J-B Wholesale
(General pet supplies)
5 Raritan Road
Oakland, NJ 07436
800-526-0388

RC Steele
(General pet supplies)
P.O. Box 910
Brockport, NY 14420-0910
800-872-3773
716-637-1408

MORE FUN AND GAMES

Agility

Agility is one of the modern dog games that has its roots in friendly training. It requires off leash control and an enthusiastic spirit on the part of both dog and owner. For more information, contact:

United States Dog Agility Association (USDAA)
P.O. Box 850955
Richardson, TX 75085
Phone: (214) 231-9700
Fax: (214) 503-0161
E-mail: info@usdaa.com

North American Dog Agility Council (NADAC)
HCR 2, Box 277
St. Maries, ID 83861
phone: (208) 689-3803
Web site: http://www.teleport.com~jhaglund

Don't let the term Non-Sporting group deceive you, all of these dogs were bred for special functions, and some of them are quite sporty! They enjoy as much mental and physical exercise as any dog.

Agility Association of Canada (AAC)
638 Wonderland Road, S.
London, Ontario
Canada N6K 1L8
Phone: (519) 473-3410

Flyball

Flyball is a fast-paced sport that requires your dog to race to a box holding a tennis ball, press a lever to release the ball, catch it and race back to you. It is wild and crazy fun! To learn more:

North American Flyball Association
Attn: Mike Randall
1342 Jeff St.
Ytsilanti, MI 48198

Canine Good Citizen Test

The Canine Good Citizen Test is a test developed by the American Kennel Club. It is used to evaluate a dog's basic manners.

KENNEL CLUBS AND REGISTRIES

American Kennel Club (AKC)

The AKC is a registry for purebred dogs and also sponsors the Canine Good Citizen test, Agility competitions, Earthdog Tests, Lure Coursing, Tracking, Herding, Field Trials and Hunting Tests, Conformation shows and Obedience Trials.

5580 Centerview Dr., Suite 200
Raleigh, NC 27606
Phone: (919) 233-9767
Fax: (919) 233-3627
E-mail: INFO@akc.org
Web site: http://www.akc.org

United Kennel Club (UKC)

The UKC is a registry for purebred dogs and sponsors Agility,

Hunting, Terrier and Obedience Trials.

100 East Kilgore Rd.
Kalamazoo, MI 49001
Phone: (616) 343-9020
Fax: (616) 343-7037

American Mixed Breed Obedience Registry (AMBOR)

205 1st St., SW
New Prague, MN 56071
Phone: (612) 758-4598

GETTING IN TOUCH WITH THE AUTHOR

For a brochure of Andrea Arden's seminars and training classes contact:

Manhattan Dog Training
Phone: (212) 213-4288
www.manhattandogtraining.com

Index